This book is a distinctive, if not unique, treatment of how the New Testament bears on ecology. While Old Testament studies are more common, little exists on the New Testament. But here we find two chapters on Jesus's Beatitudes and two on "The Lord's Prayer." Paul, James, and Revelation contribute to this rich collection as well. In addition to Bredin's perceptive exegesis, he interweaves into his exposition contemporary data on how the cosmos is changing and what he personally is doing about this, a bridge between biblical study and living ethics.

The book will be useful to readers across the spectrum and will serve as a good text in colleges, universities, and seminaries. His style is not confrontational but inviting. Each chapter ends with questions for discussion, valuable for church study groups. Highly recommended.

WILLARD M. SWARTLEY
Professor Emeritus of New Testament
Associated Mennonite Biblical Seminary

Mark Bredin brings his unique perspective as both biblical scholar and caregiver to bear on the neglected question of what significance the New Testament has for contemporary environmental issues. The result is a creative, provocative, and engaging book that should be of interest to all Christians who seek to follow Christ in a world full of injustice, facing grave threats to its ecological health. Bredin's skills as an exegete are evident on every page, but this is no mere academic study; readers will find themselves profoundly challenged and encouraged as Bredin wrestles with the implications of the Bible's radical call upon us to care for others and for the earth as God does. This clearly-written and accessible book, with helpful summaries and reflection questions at the end of each chapter, would also serve as an excellent text for a course on the Bible and the environment.

DR. JONATHAN MOO
Assistant Professor of Biblical Studies
Whitworth University, Spokane, WA

An impressive response to the ecological crisis by a New Testament scholar and caregiver. Demonstrating the earth's need, Mark Bredin convincingly argues that God is a "Cosmic Caregiver." Followers of Jesus Christ are caregivers for the earth. I highly recommend this well-informed, original, and well-written book.

DR. EDWARD P. ECHLIN
Ecological Theologian
Author of *Earth Spirituality: Jesus at the Centre*; *The Cosmic Circle: Jesus and Ecology*; *Climate and Christ: A Prophetic Alternative*.

Mark Bredin has gifted us with a persuasive portrayal of the Bible's message calling humanity without equivocation to care for the earth. Echoing the concreteness so characteristic of biblical writers, Bredin's New Testament focus complements numerous other treatments more oriented toward the Old Testament. His discussion is comprehensive. Jesus, of course, is the center but we also learn how Paul taught creation care. The reader of this book will likely be changed—Bible-believers will be challenged to care more for the environment; environmentalists will be challenged to recognize the Bible as their ally.

TED GRIMSRUD
Professor of Theology and Peace Studies
Eastern Mennonite University

I found this book to be scripturally edifying, morally compelling, and ministry equipping. As a leader in the church who cares about mobilizing Christians to care for creation, this is one of the best books I have ever read in that field. I am personally motivated by its challenges, and I am more deeply devoted to the Creator because its explanations prompt both action and awe.

DR. JOEL C. HUNTER
Senior Pastor of Northland, A Church Distributed
Longwood, Florida, USA

The Ecology of the New Testament

THE ECOLOGY OF THE NEW TESTAMENT

CREATION, RE-CREATION, AND THE ENVIRONMENT

MARK BREDIN

InterVarsity Press
P.O. Box 1400, Downers Grove, IL 60515-1426
World Wide Web: www.ivpress.com
E-mail: email@ivpress.com

©2010 by Mark Bredin

All rights reserved. No part of this book may be reproduced in any form without written permission from InterVarsity Press.

InterVarsity Press® is the book-publishing division of InterVarsity Christian Fellowship/USA®, a movement of students and faculty active on campus at hundreds of universities, colleges and schools of nursing in the United States of America, and a member movement of the International Fellowship of Evangelical Students. For information about local and regional activities, write Public Relations Dept., InterVarsity Christian Fellowship/USA, 6400 Schroeder Rd., P.O. Box 7895, Madison, WI 53707-7895, or visit the IVCF website at <www.intervarsity.org>.

All Scripture quotations, unless otherwise indicated, are taken from the New Revised Standard Version Bible, copyright 1989, Division of Christian Education of the National Council of the Churches of Christ in the United States of America. Used by permission. All rights reserved.

Scripture quotations marked NIV are taken from the THE HOLY BIBLE, NEW INTERNATIONAL VERSION®, NIV.® Copyright © 1973, 1978, 1984 by Biblica, Inc.™ Used by permission. All rights reserved worldwide.

Scripture quotations marked NASB are taken from the NEW AMERICAN STANDARD BIBLE ®, Copyright © 1960, 1962, 1963, 1968, 1971, 1972, 1973, 1975, 1977, 1995 by The Lockman Foundation. Used by permission.

Scripture quotations marked RSV are from the Revised Standard Version of the Bible, copyright 1952 [2nd edition, 1971] by the Division of Christian Education of the National Council of the Churches of Christ in the United States of America. Used by permission. All rights reserved.

Scripture quotations marked NLT are taken from the Holy Bible, New Living Translation, copyright © 1996, 2004. Used by permission of Tyndale House Publishers, Inc., Wheaton, Illinois 60189. All rights reserved.

Scripture quotations marked NJB are taken from the The New Jerusalem Bible © 1985 by Darton, Longman & Todd Ltd and Doubleday & Company, Inc.

Originally published by Biblica.

ISBN 978-0-8308-5638-1

Printed in the United States of America ∞

 InterVarsity Press is committed to protecting the environment and to the responsible use of natural resources. As a member of Green Press Initiative we use recycled paper whenever possible. To learn more about the Green Press Initiative, visit <www.greenpressinitiative.org>.

Cataloging-in-Publication Data is available through the Library of Congress.

P	17	16	15	14	13	12	11	10	9	8	7	6	5	4	3	2	1
Y	28	27	26	25	24	23	22	21	20	19	18	17	16	15	14		

I dedicate this book to Jodie, John, Molly, and Nev.

CONTENTS

Foreword	xi
Acknowledgments	xiii
Chapter 1	1
Why Care for the Earth?	
Chapter 2	13
Cosmic Justice	
Chapter 3	29
Ecology and the Wilderness	
Chapter 4	41
Jesus "with the Wild Beasts" (Mark 1:13)	
Chapter 5	47
Bad News	
Chapter 6	61
The Beatitudes 1: Matthew 5:36	
Chapter 7	71
The Beatitudes 2: Matthew 5:7–12	
Chapter 8	85
The Lord's Prayer 1: Matthew 6:9–10	
Chapter 9	97
The Lord's Prayer 2: Matthew 6:11–13	
Chapter 10	107
Food Makes the World Go Round	

Chapter 11   127
    Paul's Ecological Teaching

Chapter 12   149
    James's Ecological Teaching

Chapter 13   165
    Revelation's Ecological Teaching

Chapter 14   181
    Caregivers of Body Earth

Notes   189

Bibliography   203

FOREWORD

Recently many Christians have become aware that the Bible has something to say about creation that is relevant to our age of ecological crisis and looming ecological catastrophe. To care for the earth and to value other creatures as God does are responsibilities the biblical God has given to humanity, responsibilities we have disastrously neglected, and therefore also responsibilities that are especially compelling and urgent today. But for the most part, awareness of this ecological dimension of the Bible has been based only on a few key texts, mostly in the Old Testament. Within the New Testament writings, perhaps only Romans 8:19–23 has drawn much attention.

What Mark Bredin has shown in this book is not only that there are many other New Testament texts that refer directly and specifically to our relationship with other creatures, but very importantly, he has also shown that the ecological dimension is integral to major overall concerns of the New Testament: the kingdom of God, salvation, discipleship, justice, and hope. Well-known passages such as the Beatitudes and the Lord's Prayer turn out to be highly relevant to Bredin's theme. So is the rich seam of New Testament references to table fellowship and food.

Bredin writes about the New Testament in a way that will be readily accessible to a nonspecialist readership, but at the same time his work is rooted in sound biblical scholarship. It also reflects his strong practical commitment to the changes in lifestyle that we must all consider very seriously if his arguments are valid.

In short, this is a book that will widen the horizons within which we read Scripture. Those who think the New Testament irrelevant to contemporary concerns will have to think again. Those whose faith and discipleship have so far left the nonhuman creation out of account will be encouraged to follow Jesus into this area too. Those already convinced that care for creation is part of our calling as Christians will find that it is even more integral to the New Testament's vision of the world than they have supposed.

RICHARD BAUCKHAM
Emeritus Professor of New Testament Studies, University of St Andrews
Senior Scholar, Ridley Hall, Cambridge

ACKNOWLEDGMENTS

My biggest acknowledgment is for my wife, Fran, who, despite her own work, has carefully read through this book, reminding me that I am writing to be understood by others.

I am indebted to Richard Bauckham, who continues to be an inspiration for applying the message of Scripture to the big issues of modern life. His continued friendship moderates my own more volatile take on life.

I thank Willard Swartley and Edward Echlin, who, over the years, have engaged with the big contemporary issues relating to the whole of society in light of the Bible. They also, like Bauckham, provide a model for younger generations of Christian scholars to see Scripture as authoritative to the global issues our world faces.

I also thank Lance Stone, who commented on versions of certain chapters and whose sermons give me hope that it is possible to communicate Scripture's central message more widely.

I have been fortunate to have had lively, intelligent young people around our home who have also encouraged me with their enthusiasm for the world and its future. I want to mention in particular, my daughters, Hannah and Charis, as well as Alek and James, for their lively conversation and enthusiasm. My daughters also had the misfortune to suffer the occasional readings from the book.

I give a special mention to those students who gave up a week of their summer to attend a conference at St John's Theological College, Nottingham, which I led on ecology and the Bible. Their enthusiasm for faith, theology, and the world was a much-needed tonic in the closing stages of writing.

I also thank Paul Bishop, who at times provided stimulating discussions and made me aware of new perspectives.

I thank Eileen Turner, who, while director of Extension Studies at St John's College, Nottingham, encouraged the development of study modules relating to Scripture and the care of humans and the rest of creation. Such opportunities were indispensable to exploring the notion of care and theology together.

I am very fortunate to live in a city that is committed to developing a more sustainable way of life. I have been inspired by the Transition Cambridge Group, whose weekly newsletter has reminded me that we must be positive and act locally for our environment.

In the final stages of preparation, I enjoyed the help of one of the publisher's editors, Julia Snyder, whose patience and professional skills were much welcomed at a time when they were much needed.

Chapter 1

WHY CARE FOR THE EARTH?

Recently, a church minister asked me, "What's the point of biblical scholarship?" My reply expresses how influential biblical study has been for me: "If it had not been for biblical studies, I would not be enjoying my current job supporting people with learning disabilities, a job in which I'm paid considerably less than the UK national average. I would not have taken up my practice of growing my own food, saving water, and using less oil. I would not be living without a car or be shopping for items that have not involved the suffering of fellow humans or other living creatures."

Without biblical studies my life would be considerably different. Thinking back on my journey with God, I see that God has led me to a commitment to biblical studies that continues to transform my previous worldview dominated by greed to one based on "care." I believe that God has led me to theological study to help me see the world from his perspective.

This book is written to share some of the perspectives and visions of the New Testament that have been influential on my life.

The Task

Since the 1970s, I have heard voices proclaiming ecological doom. I am not a scientist so I have been cautious in assessing the various arguments about climate change and oil depletion. I limit my task to understanding what the New Testament has to say to us about our relationship with each other and the rest of creation. This is why this book is titled *The Ecology of the New Testament*. I use "ecology" in the sense of considering social relations as belonging to ecological relations. I see human beings as part of the natural world. I urge that we consider human relationships in the context of all creation.

I will show that God's redeeming actions in creation call Christians to see their ecological, as well as personal, sins and repent. Through repentance we learn to care for each other and the planet because the Bible says so, and not because scientists, politicians, and environmental campaigners tell us to. This does not mean that we ignore those voices, but we must certainly listen to the Bible.

This Book

I expect most readers will be Christians who are living comfortably in North America or Europe. Some may feel discontented with their lives and separated from God's good creation; others may find themselves questioning what it means to follow Christ's example in our hoarding and greedy society.

I hope this book may offer some food for thought regarding the teachings of the New Testament. Such thought should involve assessing truthfully our own culpability in the issues relating to the ecological crisis as the writing of this book has done for me. Further, I pray that the Holy Spirit leads you to seek diligently the New Testament's guidance whether you are skeptical of those calling for environmental preservation or utterly convinced it is one of the most important issues for Christians today.

I am also writing this book to myself, as I struggle to make sense of my call to follow Christ in the early decades of the third millennium.

I would not have attempted to write on this subject unless I believed it was important, indeed vital, for the practice of my faith.

God's Care for the Earth

A dominant theme throughout this book is the need to care for the earth because it is God's good creation. I believe that the neglect, abuse, and despoliation of the world damage something that is precious to God and also are an indirect, sometimes direct, cause of much of the death and suffering that people endure. The world is precious to God. This is evident throughout the Old Testament.

In Genesis 1:31 when God had finished his creation, he saw everything that he had made, and he declared, "It was very good." Elsewhere in the Bible this same creation shouts and sings for joy because God's awesome deeds include the provision of abundant crops and flowing water (Psalm 65:5–13). We read further that the presence of the Lord makes creation happy, so that the sea roars, the floods clap their hands, and the hills sing for joy (Psalm 98:7–9). The psalmist also observes that "these [all creation] all look to you to give them their food in due season; when you give to them, they gather it up; when you open your hand, they are filled with good things" (Psalm 104:27–28). God "save[s] humans and animals alike" (Psalms 36:6). He waters the trees abundantly and feeds the young lions when they call to him (104:16, 21). This psalm also recounts the wonderful harmony between God's creatures so that the grass grows for the cattle and plants for people to use (104:14–15).

Such positive views of creation stand at the heart of the Old Testament. It is also the case for the New Testament as I will demonstrate throughout this book. It is significant that in John 1:3, Jesus is said to be cocreator with God: "All things came into being through him, and without him not one thing came into being." The claim that Jesus is the cocreator of the world reiterates the intrinsic value of the planet to God such that he shows commitment to the material world by becoming incarnate with it (John 1:14; Colossians 1:16–17; Hebrews 1:3).

Closely connected to the preciousness of God's creation and the need to care for it are themes of peace and justice. These themes are central to the Old and New Testaments. The current book will be rooted in God's goal of establishing justice for creation, establishing God's peaceable kingdom on earth. Despite depressing statistics about our world, as Christians we live in the hope of God bringing eternal resurrection to all creation, an eternal and whole peace. The hope for the peaceable kingdom on earth is connected intimately with the fact that what God has created is good and made with a purpose.

In the light of the dominant theme of caring for God's creation, this book will also encourage Christians to look more deeply at their lifestyles in terms of how these cause destruction to God's good creation.

Motivations

This book is motivated in part by scientific claims that humanity is causing damage to the environment through lack of care: damage detected particularly in climate change, deforestation, desertification, loss of biodiversity, disappearing oil and clean water, and erosion of topsoil to mention a few.

As a Christian claiming that Scripture is authoritative, I am driven to make a distinctively Bible-centered contribution to the environmental debates that are so central to society's leaders and voters alike. As a New Testament specialist, if I don't take the opportunity to respond to the present ecological crisis through Scripture, I cannot complain that the Christian voice is being ignored, nor can I face the church minister and say that biblical study is important and relevant to the world.

A second motivation is the apparent neglect of full-scale studies in the New Testament of the environmental crisis. The New Testament has been neglected in this when compared to the Old Testament, which has seen a considerable number of publications. The Anglican bishop of Liverpool, James Jones, perceptively writes: "When it comes to the ethics of the environment, or what could be called an earth-ethic, Christians often turn to the pages of the Old Testament."[1] Bishop Jones adds with great honesty that "if you asked me what Jesus had to say about the earth and whether the Gospels had anything to say in formulating an environmental ethic, I would have thought 'precious little.'"[2]

However, several New Testament studies focusing on peace and justice pave the way for important applications of the New Testament to ecological issues. As far back as 1987 Perry Yoder commented that shalom and shalom making mean ecological wholeness.[3] My study is to differing degrees inspired by André Trocmé's *Jesus and the Nonviolent Revolution*, John Howard Yoder's *The Politics of Jesus*, Walter Wink's *Engaging the Powers*, Richard Hays's *The Moral Vision of the New Testament*, Willard Swartley's *Covenant of Peace*, Glen Stassen's *Living the Sermon on the Mount*, and Michael Gorman's *Reading Paul*.

Finally, I am motivated to share with you what I see as the central insights of the New Testament, especially regarding the need to care not only for fellow human brothers and sisters but also for all creation. I argue that the kingdom of peace we hope for is best established by caring for each other and the rest of creation. I believe we must develop a theology rooted in care, seeing our human existence as part of a network of relationship of which we are only a small segment.

Methodology

My approach to the New Testament will make every effort to understand the texts in their original literary and social contexts. This kind of study is generally referred to by biblical scholars as "exegesis." Through also acknowledging our own cultural and political agendas that we bring to the texts, the message of the New Testament will spring up from its pages, energizing our ministry to bring God's peaceable kingdom on earth. Much of what gets in the way of understanding the New Testament is our failure to recognize the cultural baggage we bring.

The Ecological Crisis

The extent to which humans are causing irreparable damage to the planet is open to dispute, but this book believes that planet Earth is in danger and that humans should be concerned. Many have found this hard to accept as our way of life is based on easy access to the earth's resources. The ecological crisis that scientists and environmentalists talk about can be summed up in the following points:[4]

- *Global change.* Climate changes are causing ecological devastation through flooding, droughts, and extreme weather. There is some dispute as to whether this is caused by humans. However, most politicians and scientists claim climate change is the biggest threat to our world today. Many see it as directly related to high consumption of fossil fuels on the part of the richer nations.
- *Deforestation.* The loss of forests leads to climate change as the trees' capacity to absorb greenhouse gases is lost. Soils dry out and become deserts, and habitats and species are lost—a problem for us, as a quarter of the medicines we use today are from rain forest plants. Loss of forests is driven by (a) the need to make space for cattle to satisfy appetite for beef; (b) the demand for goods made from wood (including paper products); (c) mineral and oil extraction (major oil companies like BP, Shell, and Exxon are all involved in exploiting different rain forests); and (d) hydroelectric dams to provide the necessary energy for mineral and oil extraction cause flooding of areas of forest. All deforestation can also cause displacement of indigenous peoples.
- *Loss of biodiversity.* It is said that one extinction leads to another leading to another and so on. It is thought that 10 percent of the world's species could disappear within twenty-five years because of the breakdown of the rain forest ecosystems.
- *Shortage of water.* Lack of clean water is becoming one of the biggest problems facing our world and its people.

As responsible Christians we must ask ourselves: Are our consumption habits leading to such damage? We should not let our political positions and cultural upbringing alone lead us to take a pro- or anti-environmentalist perspective. We must listen to the New Testament carefully and thoughtfully whether we vote Republican or Democrat.

And wherever our cultural sensitivities lie, we must make those elected to positions of power know our concern for the planet because of our Christian faith.

Christians and Environmental Preservation

Many Christians see environmental preservation as unimportant. Their position is rooted in seeing God's redemptive actions as being human centered. Yet human-centered readings of the Bible say more about our Western technological mindset than about the Bible's message.

Salvation History Means Salvation Ecology

Barbara Rossing, a leading New Testament scholar, quotes one Christian writer exemplifying a view of God and the Bible that is far from caring for God's good creation: "God gave us the earth. We have dominion over the plants, the animals, the trees. God said: 'Earth is yours. Take it. Rape it. It's yours.'"[5]

Some Christians see the central teaching of the New Testament as redemption from imminent judgment for only an elect few. This redemption excludes most of the world's population, as well as the rest of creation. Therefore, the natural world cannot be the object of particular ethical concern. The natural world is seen as providing only the background to the greater drama of God's redemptive actions to bring the elect of humankind to salvation, which is seen as a process of emancipation from nature.

Many of us, including Christians who are actively involved in environmental preservation, hold the above view that salvation is only for humanity. Why is such a view so dominant, and does it have a basis in the New Testament?

I believe this view comes out of an individualistic human-centered reading of the New Testament. It is important for today's Christians to consider that the New Testament writers presupposed the importance of all creation and not just humans. Unlike modern Westerners, the people of the New Testament did not live in distinct communities separated from the soil, flora, and animals; they recognized their need to care for the land around them as well as their livestock. Such a worldview was also central to the Old Testament writers. The New Testament writers were so familiar with their environment they did not feel any urgency to spell out what was very obvious to them but what is not so obvious to us.

However, having said this it is important that we recognize in our reading of the Bible how it recounts human sinful actions. I want to share with you a reflection I had recently on the Tower of Babel story.

Escape from the Tower of Babel

The Tower of Babel narrative (Genesis 11) describes how humanity united by one language builds a tower to reach the heavens. As humans attempt to build toward heaven, they come to imagine that they are like gods, and this hubris is ultimately the cause of destruction and wars. It does not take a huge leap of the imagination to see the parallels between our modern era and the era that produced the Babel story.

I want to share with you my reflection on this story:

> I found myself high in the tower with others. We were all so desperate to escape. Why? We were dying because we had separated ourselves from the rest of creation below us. In our panic we fled. Rapidly we descended the steep outside steps of the tower. As we did so, we eagerly kept before us signs of land below like sailors looking for the first sign of land after a long sea journey. Our descent was hasty and driven by the need to be reunited with the land, in Hebrew *'adamah* from which we humans are named *'adam*. This is the land that we had so eagerly fled from in our building of the tower to reach heaven. Alarmingly in our descent we soon discovered that we were getting no closer to the earth; we couldn't see it; there was no sign—we had gone too far from the earth we are named after, and it was too late to return. Tragically many preferred to throw themselves

from the tower rather than remaining in the tower with no hope of returning to earth.

Underlying my reflection on the Babel story is modern humanity's story. Humanity in seeking to separate itself from the rest of creation is motivated to do so because of its wish to be independent. Fallen humanity doesn't like the idea of being "part of the rest of creation." Rather, humans seek to be godlike, to "make a name for themselves;" in other words, they want to live as though they were creators and not created. Putting space between them and the rest of creation somehow gives them the illusion of being in control and above it. But it is an illusion, for humanity cannot live without the rest of creation.

God as a Caregiver

Thinking of God as a "caregiver" has helped me understand more the God I encounter in the Bible. My own work as a "caregiver" has been influential. In this section I hope to introduce you to this not-so-well-known idea of God.

What comes to mind when we think about God? What we think about God says a lot about how we see ourselves and influences how we act. Christians often support their idea of God with their favorite bits of the Bible. For example, some see God as a warrior figure to justify going to war or even to plunder the earth's resources.

It is very important that we don't use the Bible to justify our own human views and prejudices that conveniently ignore the God who clothes the grass of the field and feeds the birds of the air and who cares for others more than he cares for himself. I suggest that we keep in mind the Bible's dominant depiction of God as one who is active in the daily life of his creation. Creation is valuable to God, and therefore God is driven to care for it and to prevent those who harm it from destroying what he made. God is not an aloof figure—a clock maker who, after making it, stops caring about it.

God's relationship with creation is as one whose whole being is invested in his work. If we focus on the God of the Bible—one who is intimately connected with what he has made—then we will be critical of a vision that sees God as a despotic landlord instead of filling the more caring role represented in images traditionally associated with mother, gardener, or nurse. God of the Bible, I believe, is as much like a caregiver as he is a modern president or royal figure.

I don't wish to make God into our buddy. It is biblically true that God is Creator and that we are created. Yet while God is "in heaven" (Matthew 6:9), he is also the Father of all creation (Matthew 6:9). There are many descriptions and metaphors in the Bible relating to God that emphasize more the intimate God who knows his creation by name. Images such as shepherd and gardener, for example, express the caring and compassionate God. In this tradition I want to offer the metaphor of God as a "caregiver" because I think it advocates the downstairs (servant) God over and against the upstairs (aristocratic) God.

I previously argued for this in an article in 2008 on the book of Revelation.[6] The initial worries some had with my argument were that I neglect the authoritative otherness of God. My response is that anyone who has been in the care of a skilled caregiver will recognize his or her utter dependence on that person, an experience I had while in intensive care after a cycling accident. Here, I became dependent on the nurses and doctors. The more vulnerable the person is, the more authoritative the carer becomes; yet a good caregiver takes charge in such a way that gives security and communicates confidence to the vulnerable person.

This is what Jesus means when he says that the great among you must be servants. The caregiver is an image that many may identify with, especially anyone who has cared for children, elderly relatives, or even a plot of land. Furthermore, such a metaphor fits closely the depictions of God in Scripture as I hope to show in this book.

Summary of *The Ecology of the New Testament*

In this book, I argue that we must care for the earth because the Bible reveals God as one who cares for it, because he created it, and we are called to show our love by serving him through caring for what he has made. It has been too easy to neglect particularly the New Testament in terms of the ecological crisis. If we publicly declare, "Jesus is Lord," then Jesus's life and teachings must drive us constantly to serve him in our world, and we must read the New Testament in our context of ecological crisis. When we unpack the New Testament's ecological message about caring for the earth, we will find that the New Testament speaks to the life-threatening, violent imperialism and tribalism lying at the heart of the ecological crisis, but with an invigorating hope for God's completion of his creation. It is this hope that drives the Christian to care for God's creation.

Jesus of Nazareth provides a vision of God's future when his will is to be done on earth as in heaven. The New Testament documents God's re-creating actions as he works to establish his future reign of cosmic justice on earth. At the heart of the New Testament is its teaching "to love God with all our being" and "our neighbors as ourselves." It is evident in all the teachings found in the New Testament that "to love God" is "to love what God has made," and according to the respective gifts God has given each, we must act to show that love toward all God's creation. The New Testament teaches us how this must be expressed. Further, it points toward truer sources of joy and fulfilment that lie in generosity and mercy, fundamental characteristics of God. It provides a vision of cosmic justice rooted in future reality where God's dwelling will be on earth.

Chapter Summary

This chapter has introduced the main themes and hopes of *The Ecology of the New Testament*. Human rebellion against God is seen in the mistreatment of God's creation revealed most powerfully for us today in environmental damage. This arises through greed and the desire for self-empowerment regardless of how this affects the rest of creation. God is not a careless superpower separated from the sufferings of his creation. God is the caregiver who enters into his contract with his creation to bring it to completion as he intended.

Reflection Questions

1. What comes to mind when you think of the New Testament and the environmental crisis?
2. Which aspects of the New Testament inspire you in thinking about the environmental crisis?
3. Which aspects have you found problematic, and why?

Chapter 2

COSMIC JUSTICE

Seek first his kingdom and justice.—Matthew 6:33

If you have men who will exclude any of God's creatures from the shelter of compassion and pity, you will have men who deal likewise with their fellow men.—St. Francis of Assisi (1181-1226)[1]

Social justice without ecological justice is injustice which ultimately injures people badly.—Edward Echlin[2]

My Body and Body Earth

Throughout my childhood I loved running. When I pushed myself too hard, my body would tell me, at times quite painfully. Yet I was trained as an athlete to ignore aches and pains. I was taught to see my physical body as an enemy that needed conquering. Unfortunately, such a dualistic attitude toward my body resulted in serious injury. If I were to continue running, I needed to learn to listen to those aches and pains. I slowly turned to a more sustainable approach to running, and I felt health and exhilaration while running because I cared for my body. In order for my body to stay healthy, my mind had to heed all aches and pains.

I have started to see this growing relationship with my physical body as a model for a relationship with the wider body, earth. The earth is in many ways the wider body of the human community. Sadly, our earth, our green beautiful earth, is in danger like our personal bodies. Further, like our bodies, the earth is telling us so. It is important that we learn to listen to our body "earth" and where it is suffering. We must not ignore it as I was inclined to do with running in my younger competitive days. We must learn to adopt a lifestyle that cares for our body "earth." We must seek to do activities that are good for the earth such as running is for the body. We must not see the earth as an enemy from which we must extract every drop of blood it can produce. Such a way leads to catastrophe on a level that makes my painful running injuries seem microscopic in proportion.

If our physical hearts are weak, the flow of our life is slowed. As we become fully aware of this danger, we take action to heal our hearts so that we can live more wholly. Likewise we must develop awareness and sensitivity to our wider body, the earth. If the ozone layer around our earth were to disappear for even an instant, we would die. If the sun were to stop shining, the flow of life would stop. We must make every effort to respond to our wider body as we would if we were told that our physical heart were sick. We must do justice not only to our individual bodies, but also to our larger body, earth. If we don't, it will become sicker and our individual bodies along with it. Therefore personal and social justice must include ecological justice. I call this holistic justice "cosmic justice."

Health for All Creation

God's "justice" in the Old Testament is rooted in concern for the well-being and salvation of humanity. However, this justice also implies well-being and salvation for all God's creation.

Such a view is not obvious to many twenty-first-century Westerners who generally presuppose distinctions between social and ecological justice, putting much greater emphasis on the social. We often find it difficult to understand justice as something that extends to the whole earth. I argue that we must make a conscious effort to align ourselves with the whole earth. This chapter firmly supports international ethicist and theologian Michael Northcott, who rightly observes that the biblical narrative of justice suggests that justice is ecologically situated and not just relating to humanity.[3]

The Old Testament in Three Words

We cannot understand the New Testament without the Old Testament, which can be summed up in three words: creation, fall, and re-creation. These words provide the key for understanding the Bible. We should read the Old Testament as one book recording the story of God's activity of redeeming creation.

Creation

God declared his whole creation "good"; this did not mean only humankind but all creation.[4] The psalmist, for example, writes: "You save humans and animals alike, O LORD" (Psalm 36:6). All creation is intrinsically valuable in the eyes of the Creator. Christopher Wright says, "God provides the same food for us as for the rest of the animals (Genesis 1:29–30). . . . We, along with all other animals, have the same basic needs of food, water, sleep, and shelter. So then we are animals among animals."[5] Humans and animals alike share the breath of life (Genesis 1:30; 6:17; 7:15, 22; cf. Psalm 104:29–30). Those of us who arrogantly think that humanity is more important to God than the rest of creation should recall that humanity is not the first to be created, and we don't even get our own day of creation. Wright emphasizes, "It is easy to say that human beings are superior, or unique, or special. Undoubtedly so. But the opening chapters of the Bible do not immediately emphasize human uniqueness. On the contrary, it seems that at point after point the Bible tells us that we have more in common with the rest of creation than in distinction from it."[6] [FN: Wright, 117].

Prolific writer and Kentucky agrarian Wendell Berry reminds us that humans are children of Adam and that the Hebrew word *'adam* means "dirt."[7] Therefore, humans are beings of the land and not marked out as superior. As children of Adam, we are connected to the soil, and human life is to interact with the earth.

Fall

After creation came the fall. The fall is neglected by many Christians who are embarrassed by talk of being "sinners." It is more "modern" to be positive about humanity. However, I believe we cannot understand the Bible's depiction of God without the fall from which God is seeking to redeem us.

One result of the fall the Old Testament depicts is humankind setting itself over the rest of creation (Genesis 4:8–16; 6:5–7; 11:1–9). Humans begin to see the rest of creation as something to control and tame. It seems to me that even to think of social and ecological justices as "separate" is to read Scripture through unredeemed eyes. Scripture does not see humans as separated and above the rest of God's creation. We are "dirt people." Fundamental to the climactic fall story of Babel is how humans deny that they are "adam"—by building a tower to separate themselves from the dirt that sustains them.

Biblically speaking, because of the fall we have become enemies of the land (Genesis 3:17). Wendell Berry illustrates this aspect of the fall in the way modern factory agriculture treats the soil as a lifeless matrix: "The modern farm is understood as a surface on which various mechanical operations are performed, and to which various chemicals are applied. The under-surface of reality of organisms and roots is mostly ignored."[8]

As a keen carer of a small rented patch of land in Cambridge, England, I certainly see that the way we treat the land is akin to the way we treat others and our own personal bodies. If I treat the land with chemicals, not seeing it as a living thing, I will soon reduce its health so that it will not produce what I need. It becomes unhealthy, and therefore I become unhealthy and others become sick.

Redemption (Re-creation)

The word "redemption" is an important one for Christians. "Redemption" (buying back from slavery) is one of several theological shorthand terms describing God as acting to re-create his fallen creation. Throughout this book I prefer to spell out what I mean by "redemption" and "redeeming" using the words "re-creation" and "re-creating." The Old Testament narrative is dominated by "re-creating" in which God works toward re-creating his good creation, which was and is damaged by the human fall. In this "re-creation" God reveals to humanity what cosmic justice means.

Wendell Berry compares this "re-created" vision to "soil husbandry," which understands the soil as a living community of creatures. All of us, including crops and animals, are members of the soil community.[9]

Often when I have been in an area of land that has been well cared for, I am struck not only by the healthy sound of bird song, the buzz of bees, and rich signs of biodiversity, but also by the healthiness of human relationships. This is in contrast to the human relationships I observe when stuck in traffic jams, and there are a lot of them in Cambridge! The cared-for land is more a vision of "re-creation" than being stuck in a traffic jam.

Summary

We live between the fall of creation and its re-creation, anticipating and hoping for God's completion of his re-creating work. However, we are limited and perceive partially because of our human-centered ways of seeing God's creation. The Old Testament provides us with a God-centered way of seeing. We increasingly have glimpses of the effects our fallen state has caused. Isaiah, for example, commenting on the wickedness of Judea writes what has led to the land lying desolate and the cities burned (Isaiah 1:7). Revelation similarly reveals how plagues are the result of human sin (Revelation 6:15–17). Humans must learn to repent, not only for themselves but also for the sake of the rest of God's creation.

Effects of Separating Social from Ecological Justice

Humanity's disobedience to God's law has had serious consequences for the earth. I believe that the law given to Moses on Mount Sinai is not unlike what running is to the body if done well. The law, like running, makes us aware of the voice of the body (earth) we rely on. Humanity has failed to understand how important all creation is to God. More, it has caused profound damage to creation. Ruth Valerio writes:

> Where disobedience to God leads to social injustice, there the land will fail and become desolate and fruitless. The importance of this truth for today can hardly be denied, as the greed and idolatry of globalisation trample over human beings and destroy the rest of creation. It is now almost universally acknowledged that environmental and social issues, far from being in competition, have to be tackled together.[10]

These words are illustrated in the well-documented fact that the land, rivers, and lakes of the poor are the dumping grounds of the rich. In the United States, close to 85 percent of all toxic landfills are in neighbourhoods composed of the marginalized. Native American reservations often agree to accept landfill waste as a means to increase their income, sometimes with life-threatening consequences.[11]

Promisingly, over the last few decades we have started to use the phrase "ecological justice" as we become increasingly sensitized to our consumption patterns and their harming effects on the environment. As United Nations Agenda 21 states: "The major cause of continued deterioration of the global environment is the unsustainable pattern of consumption and production, particularly in the industrialized countries which is a matter of grave concern aggravating poverty and imbalances."[12]

A few modern examples will help illustrate this point.

Chocolate, Wood, Coffee, and Water

The way we consume in North America and Europe affects others. In this subsection I focus on chocolate, wood, coffee, and water to demonstrate how the way we acquire these imports brings suffering to other humans as well as the wider environment.

Chocolate. In the leading international environmental magazine, the *Ecologist*, Andrew Wasley writes: "Virtually everything we buy—food, clothing, household appliances or holidays, comes with an ecological price-tag."[13]

Chocolate, for example, is so much part of our daily diet in developed nations, yet so few of us know that children in western Africa are sometimes sold into slave labor or forced to work under inhumane conditions and extreme abuse in cocoa farms harvesting the beans from which chocolate is made.[14]

Wood. In *Business Ethics* April 2010 it was reported that

> deforestation continues to be one of the world's biggest environmental problems, especially in fast developing regions like South America, Southeast Asia and Africa. Cutting down large numbers of trees erodes land and silts waterways, displaces native people and wildlife, and releases tons of carbon dioxide (which is stored in living wood fiber) into the atmosphere, contributing to global warming.[15]

As a British citizen I was concerned to read Andrew Wasley in the *Ecologist* regarding the UK and wood consumption:

> British consumers appear to be addicted to cheap timber and blind to the chain of abuses that lie behind many timber products. Each weekend thousands queue up to purchase tables, chair, cabinets, blinds and other similar, seemingly innocent and unremarkable items, much linked to conflict, corruption and human rights abuses.[16]

Coffee and Water. Coffee is the United States' second largest import, behind oil. The United States also consumes one-fifth of the world's coffee.[17] Because coffee is a water-intensive commodity, our addiction to coffee means that the demand for water is shifted from the place of consumption, North America and Europe, to the place of production, often Africa or Latin America.

It costs about 21,000 liters (4,619 gallons) of water to produce 1 kilogram (2.2 pounds) of roasted coffee. For a standard cup of coffee we require 7 grams of roasted coffee, so that a cup of coffee costs 140 liters (30 gallons) of water. Assuming that a standard cup of coffee is 125 milliliters, we thus need more than 1,100 drops of water to produce 1 drop of coffee. Altogether, the world population requires about 120 billion cubic meters of water per year in order to be able to drink coffee. International trade in coffee products is responsible for 80 billion cubic meters of virtual water exports, which is about 6 percent of the international virtual water flow in the world.[18]

Coffee drinkers do not cover the environmental and social costs that are often associated with the use and pollution of water in the exporting regions. We who are coffee drinkers perhaps should know how much our coffee costs the environment and the people who help produce it; statistics suggest that the producers often receive less than the price it takes to produce.[19]

Summary. If we ignore the rights of other humans, as well as the rest of creation, we experience cosmic injustice and our body, earth, suffers. Therefore, the present ecological crisis calls us to think beyond our own interests and rather to perceive our existence as part of a wider network of relationships including the rain forests, rivers, and sky. The examples of chocolate, wood, coffee, and water show how there is suffering because of our assumption that we have a right to anything we want. There are also many other examples. Too often, we are like sleepwalkers, not knowing what we are doing or where we are heading. The Old Testament records how God is waking us from our sleep and inviting us to see the consequences of our actions so that we can repent.

Cosmic Justice and the Old Testament

In the Apostles' Creed we acknowledge our belief in God as "maker of heaven and earth." As God is Creator of all, it follows that God's justice is not divided between social and ecological justice.

Social and Ecological Justice

Northcott expresses the cosmic nature of justice as follows:

> Justice in the Old Testament is cosmic and not just personal. Human actions which mirror divine justice affirm and sustain the wholeness of creation, while human injustice causes oppression and misery not only among the children of men but among the beasts of the field and trees on the mountains.[20]

The major Hebrew and Greek words for justice occur over one thousand times in the Bible (e.g., Deuteronomy 16:20; Isaiah 61:8).[21] Chris Marshall sums up: "Biblical justice touches on every aspect of life—the personal and the social, the public and the private, the political and the religious, the human and the non-human."[22]

Peace in the Old Testament

Closely connected with justice is the idea of "peace" (see, e.g., Psalm 72:3–4). The Hebrew word for "peace," *shalom*, occurs well over two hundred times in the Old Testament, and this relates to wholeness, completeness, well-being, peace, justice, and prosperity.[23] Perry Yoder understandably prefers to use the term "shalom justice" when referring to God's re-creative actions in transforming conditions of need and oppression into ones where shalom can be found. Shalom justice equates social and ecological justice. Shalom—material and spiritual well-being—is God's ultimate goal for creation. However, I will use the phrase "cosmic justice" for sake of clarity to refer to the state of well-being and wholeness that God intended for his re-created world. Justice that is not "cosmic" is not justice in any way that we find in the Old Testament. Rather, limited justice is injustice.

The Promised Land

The Bible documents God's re-creative actions in seeking to establish cosmic justice on earth. God chooses a poor and oppressed people to stand as witnesses to an alternative society in contrast to the mighty empire Egypt. God brings Israel out of Egypt to make a covenant with it and reveals the nature of God's cosmic justice so that Israel can enact and embody it in the world.

The laws that God gives Moses enable Israel to experience and exercise cosmic justice. In the Mosaic law, cosmic justice involves social and ecological justice. God's justice refers not only to his saving justice granted to individual believers, but also to the beauty and order of his whole work, which itself witnesses to God's justice and calls us to seek it.[24] Thus God through Israel shows the world an alternative way of justice that contravenes the values of Pharaoh's justice.

Social Justice. In choosing to deliver Israel from injustice, God shows a preference for the economically, socially, and physically oppressed, for example, Israel. Israel is to form a people who show justice as taught in the commandments given to Moses. Many of those commandments relate to people. God gives to Israel so that Israel may be God's agent of mercy to all nations, so that generosity and equality become realities. This is in contrast to Pharaoh's Egypt, which exemplified oppression and abuse of power.[25]

Later, Micah proclaims that God's people are to do good through loving kindness and walking humbly before God (Micah 6:8). Micah's words relate to behavior toward the marginalized in society (6:9–12). Hillary Marlow comments that this simple statement encapsulates the whole Old Testament's vision for right relationships among and between humankind.[26] What matters for God's justice are relationships of peace as in Isaiah 11:6–9.

Isaiah similarly condemns social injustice, saying that for those who treat others harshly, their prayers, however fervent, will remain unheard and unanswered (1:11–15).[27] Specifically Isaiah says that God's people are to treat the marginalized with compassion (1:17).

Likewise, Amos attacks the rich for their oppression of the poor, as well as their lives of luxury (4:1). God's people are condemned for relying on their wealth, believing it to be a sign of God's favor and thereby treating others with contempt. The rich are guilty of abusing their privileged positions and of indifference or arrogance toward others.

Ecological Justice. The psalmist emphasizes God's concern for not only humans but also the whole of creation: "Even the sparrow finds a home, and the swallow a nest for herself, where she may lay her young, at your altars, O LORD of hosts, my King and my God" (Psalm 84:3). Similarly Psalm 72 looks for environmental well-being as a byproduct of a just and benevolent government.[28] In the same psalm there will be order and prosperity in the nature realm for the just/righteous king (cf. Isaiah 32:15–20 and 11:1–9). The king is not "just" because he adopts a human measure of justice, but because the manner of the king's rule is in conformity with God's eternal cosmic justice. When the king loves justice, the land itself and all the creatures that dwell in it prosper. When the king and the court neglect justice, the people suffer and the land suffers with them.[29] Likewise, the vision of "re-creation" in Isaiah 11:1–9 is rooted in a cosmically just government establishing global environmental concord. In this vision we see a time when there will be peace and well-being between even the wolf and the lamb.

Cosmic Covenant. Robert Murray emphasizes the link between social injustice and ecological devastation in the Old Testament, detecting in many texts an intricate web of relatedness between God, humanity, and the rest of creation.[30] He argues convincingly with considerable evidence that the rituals and laws of the covenant community of Israel are designed to preserve and restore order to the whole of damaged creation. Humanity rebels against this covenant, breaking the laws established by God, and this, as we have seen above, results in ecological crisis.

In my personal reflection on running at the beginning of this chapter, I tried to convey, by using the analogy of caring for the human body, that if we abuse our bodies we harm our spiritual and mental stability. If we break basic laws about exercising, eating healthily, and sleeping, we become unhealthy. Likewise, if we treat the planet badly by disobeying laws of restraint, we damage our body "earth." Murray's observations about the intricate links between the covenant and care for the wider body "earth" tie in with my own reflection. I believe we must ask God to help us to treat the earth well as our wider body.

An important text for Murray is the covenant with Noah recorded in Genesis 9:8–12, 16. God establishes this covenant with all creation after the flood. Murray calls this a "cosmic covenant," emphasizing the importance of creation as good and belonging to God. God promises that never again will such chaos occur, nor will he abandon his creation again. This is a covenant with all creation, in which God binds himself to humans and all other life-forms simultaneously.

In the next section we will see how God's covenant through Moses requires a way of life that is sensitive to all creation. This way of life would result in harmony as imagined in the vision of peace in Isaiah 11:6–9.

Jubilee Laws

André Trocmé sums up Jubilee laws as found in the Old Testament:[31]

- Every seventh year the land was to lie fallow. But by a special blessing of Yahweh, the land would produce a double harvest during the sixth year.
- During the seventh year all debts between Hebrews would be canceled.
- After six years of slavery every Hebrew slave was to be set free by his master.
- Every forty-nine years each family was to regain possession of the land and houses it had lost in the meantime.

Jubilee People

Central to Jubilee as set out in Leviticus 25 is to trust God for the graciousness of his mercy. The basis of Jubilee laws is that the formerly afflicted nation of Israel must now live as God's anointed, proclaiming good news to those who remain afflicted by releasing them from their respective afflictions.

The Jubilee laws demand expropriating the lands of the wealthy and liquidating the usurious system by which the ruling class has prospered.[32] Such Jubilee action means removing those things that have kept the afflicted in their poverty such as debt, prison, disabilities, and oppression. What God requires of Israel reflects what he desires for humanity; namely, broadly equitable distribution of the resources of the earth, especially land, and a curb on the tendency to accumulation with its inevitable oppression and alienation.

So Jubilee recalls that creation is God's gift. Jubilee attacks aspects of human society that have resulted in depriving other humans of that gift. Practically this means Israel was to share creation and not to hoard. Israel had inherited land, but it would be taken away if Israel did not keep the covenant.[33] In this understanding land has intrinsic worth. Land is not to be owned by rich people simply to make money from rent. On the contrary, families need land to sustain them. The land also needs the toil and labor of the community to care for it and preserve its fertility.

Why then do we assume that the Jubilee laws are simply about God's concern for humanity? There is no reason other than our myopic way of seeing the world. Remember the second key word for understanding the Old Testament: the fall. I don't believe there is any reason we place humanity above the rest of creation other than sinful thinking resulting from the fall.

Resting the Land

According to Leviticus 25:4–7, resting the land every seventh year was vital. One reason for this was that Israel needed to remember that the land belonged to God and that they needed to trust God to provide for their necessary needs. In doing so the Israelites were to live as they had lived in the wilderness for forty years, relying on God for their daily sustenance. Israel was never to forget that the fertility of the land arose from God's care for nature rather than simply through human manipulation (see Deuteronomy 8:11–18).[34] Northcott writes:

> The Sabbath of the land has ecological value, particularly for the kind of land the Hebrews were farming, which was fragile. Overtilling and overcropping by livestock resulted in soil erosion and eventual desertification, or the kind observed and condemned by the prophets as the consequence of the abuse of land by rich landowners.[35]

Similarly, Wendell Berry appreciates God's Jubilee commandments as revealing cosmic justice. For Berry the notion of "the land as gift" is pivotal. We live at enmity with the rest of creation because of the fall. We treat the land as though it were a machine that we can control and make do what we want. Yet creation is not "our" machine but is a living being that God takes joy in.

Jubilee reveals in its commandments the importance of caring for those around us and the environment that nourishes us. The Jubilee points us toward a re-created order where the polarization between humanity and the rest of creation will no longer exist. God intends humans to be in creation and not apart from it. If we treat the land as if it were our enemy, then soil erosion and eventual desertification will follow. I believe that the Jubilee law regarding the resting of the land takes us back to the teaching that the land belongs to God and that it is upon God we trust for the miracle of the land's plenty.

In sum, Jubilee instructs humans to cultivate and relate to the land, not to destroy or tame it, but to mature it, to allow it to nourish us. This is the creational role of the earth and the creational task of humanity.

Summary

God's covenant witnesses to the relation between cosmic order and human order, allowing all life to pursue and develop as God intended.[36] In God's covenant, particularly as stated in the Jubilee laws, God required Israel to reflect what he wanted for his creation: equitable distribution of the resources of the earth, especially land, and a curb on the tendency to accumulation with its inevitable oppression and alienation. Christopher Wright comments: "The jubilee thus stands as a critique not only of massive private accumulation of land and related wealth, but also of large-scale forms of collectivism or nationalization that destroy any meaningful sense of personal or family ownership."[37]

Chapter Summary

The Old Testament never conceived of social justice as separated from care for the land. Modern human technological developments have supported ideas that humanity can control and separate itself from nature. Fortunately, today, for the first time in human history, we are beginning to recognize that our technological developments are causing the extinction of many life-forms and affecting humans, particularly the poorest, youngest, and most vulnerable. The ecological crisis of modern times allows us to see what the Old Testament naturally assumes: that caring for our fellow brothers and sisters also means caring for the rest of creation, not only because of human necessity but also because it matters to God.

At the beginning of this chapter I shared with you my passion for running. In order to keep running, I obey certain laws that allow me to care for my body. In my early years I abused running by pushing myself too hard, and I did not listen to my body. My body became ill and I was unable to run. Today, we must learn to care for our wider body "earth" and not relate to it as though all that matters is that we get from it what we want, right now. If we mistreat our body "earth" this way, it will become sick just like my own body did.

Reflection Questions

1. How might distributing land to the landless help the land to be more fruitful?
2. How might God's concern for the economically poor influence our paradigm for Christian ministry regarding the ecological crisis today?
3. How can we distribute God's creation and give in a way that facilitates receivers' supporting and caring for the planet?

Chapter 3

ECOLOGY AND THE WILDERNESS

Jesus's time in the wilderness has never, until recently, struck me as particularly important for our ecologically troubled times. There are at least three obvious reasons for this: (1) I have never really experienced being in a wilderness area for more than a few hours; (2) I have never had to face a night on my own in an open space with dangerous animals; and (3) my worldview tends to be orientated toward humans. I am very much a child of the urban sprawl.

I am challenged by William Loader's claim that Jesus's lifestyle was learned in the wilderness. Also insightful is Seán McDonagh's observation that "it was during this sojourn in the desert that Jesus came to accept and appreciate the messianic ministry he was about to embrace. In order to be fully open and receptive to his call, Jesus forsook the company of people and spent time with the wild animals in the wilderness."[1] I am also influenced by Wendell Berry, who argues that the wilderness is instructive because it reveals the limits of human control.[2] He writes of the wilderness as a place "where we must go to be reborn—to receive the awareness, at once humbling and exhilarating, grievous and joyful, that we are part of Creation, one with all that we live from and all that, in turn, lives from us."[3]

In view of these insights I devote the next two chapters to Jesus's time in the desert, where he learned of God's intentions for his ministry and realized that his ministry depended on his trust in God. In the wilderness Jesus experiences God's concern for all creation, of which humanity is only a part.

Finally, we must also consider Jesus's wilderness period alongside the three key words we discussed in the last chapter: creation, fall, and re-creation. A consequence of the fall is humanity's wish to be separate from the rest of creation so that it can use it for its own selfish ends. Wilderness represents the rest of creation and is a significant place for God's re-creating work, as through it he reveals to humanity its creaturely nature.

Driven into the Wilderness

The first thing Jesus does after his baptism is to go to the wilderness. Jesus does not go to the metropolis, the center of human civilization far from the dirt. He goes where most humans don't go and where a lot of people fear to go: the wilderness. Here Jesus learns about the following:

- Establishing God's reign of cosmic justice on earth
- Trusting God
- Freeing and healing the needy and afflicted
- Attitudes toward power and success
- Human fears of suffering

Kenneth Leech sums up the importance of the wilderness:

> The essential fact to grasp is that in the desert we live by trust and by naked faith. All props, all nonessentials, all luxuries, are taken away. The desert road is one of solitude and emptiness, and it exhausts the soul. It is the place of both sterility and of the divine presence, of demons and of the encounter with God.[4]

The wilderness is not the center of human civilization but is the very place our ancestors who built the Tower of Babel wanted to avoid (Genesis 11).

Israel's time in the wilderness is significant to our understanding of Jesus's experiences in the wilderness. Exodus recounts how Israel had to leave Egypt, the epitome of ancient civilization, for the wilderness, where it could learn God's kingdom values. The wilderness is a place that God uses to teach Israel what it means to be God's special people.

Israel Learned about God in the Wilderness

God brought Israel into the wilderness so that it might learn how to become his special people and witness to the nations. In this place Israel learns of its vulnerability and need for God. Deuteronomy 8:2–3 illustrates this:

> Remember the long way that the LORD your God has led you these forty years in the wilderness, in order to humble you, testing you to know what was in your heart, whether or not you would keep his commandments. He humbled you by letting you hunger, then by feeding you with manna, with which neither you nor your ancestors were acquainted, in order to make you understand that one does not live by bread alone, but by every word that comes from the mouth of the LORD.

Egypt

To understand the wilderness place, we must understand what its opposite, Egypt, represents. Ellen Davis writes:

> The Deuteronomist aptly names Egypt "the Iron Furnace" (Deuteronomy 4:20), for it is the biblical archetype of the industrial society: burning, ceaseless in its demand for slave labor (the cheapest fuel for the ancient industrial machines), consuming until it is itself consumed in the

confrontation between divinized Pharaoh and the God of the Burning Bush.⁵

Terence Fretheim claims the plagues are ecological signs that arise from Pharaoh's sinful actions against creation.⁶ God does not take vengeance; rather, he allows Pharaoh's actions to unfold in such a way that they bring disaster to his land and people. Pharaoh's punishment is related to his sin. The Egyptians, for example, had used the Nile as a deadly instrument for genocide in killing every newborn Hebrew. Now, the same element is turned against them, and water will eventually deliver the deadly blow that will seal their destiny.⁷ Pharaoh devours the slave community and the produce of creation until the land is reduced to waste.⁸ God leaves Pharaoh to suffer the natural consequences of his actions against creation.

The Wilderness

In the wilderness Israel learns how to live according to God's standards of cosmic justice. Simply put, the law requires Israel to act in the knowledge that the whole of creation is God's (Exodus 19:5). This knowledge calls Israel to act with justice and mercy toward each other because all belongs to God. God intends the Israelites to form a people who will be bearers of God's healing intentions to all the afflicted. Christopher Wright observes the impressive breadth of situations covered by the law: protection of the poor, strangers, widows, orphans, and enemies; payment of wages; and, significantly, "even care for animals, domestic and wild, and for fruit trees."⁹ God calls Israel to be different and holy; God's people are to be his witnesses, transforming creation from Egyptian-style oppression and greed to patterns where cosmic justice reigns.

At the end of their wilderness time, God promises Israel land, as part of a community based on egalitarian principles. In this land there will be no poor. Jesuit scholar Norbert Lohfink writes:

> Yahweh intends that Israel be a nation of sisters and brothers in which there will be no more poor (cf. Deuteronomy

15:24). This in itself makes clear that, according to the Bible, the poor of Egypt are to become, through the Exodus, a kind of divinely-willed contrast-society.[10]

Numbers 26:52–56, for example, portrays a system of dividing up the land so that every tribe would have an amount proportionate to its numerical size. Each tribe, clan, and family should have sufficient land according to its size and needs. Land was not to be concentrated in the hands of the king or a wealthy few.[11]

The Promised Land is to be a microcosm of what God wants for his whole creation. In the wilderness Israel learns to love and serve only God so that it can live out the fact that all creation belongs to God. It is a sin to treat unjustly anything that God has created.

Jesus Learned in the Wilderness

Many of us are familiar with Satan's temptation of Jesus. Jesus's three wilderness temptations are highly significant in understanding Jesus. His loyalty to God in the wilderness was tested by hunger (Matthew 4:3), physical dangers (Matthew 4:6), and the temptation to fall into idolatry (Matthew 4:9). At the heart of the three temptations is the Devil's challenge to Jesus's filial obedience, trying to cause Jesus to stumble from God's will for his creation.

In the previous chapter we considered God's intent in the Old Testament to re-create his world based on cosmic justice. I am particularly struck by Isaiah's choice of words to describe God's Promised Land, words that Jesus would have been only too aware of in his wilderness period: "Then justice will dwell in the wilderness, and righteousness abide in the fruitful field. The effect of righteousness will be peace [shalom], and the result of righteousness [justice], quietness and trust forever" (Isaiah 32:16–17).

I want now to consider Jesus's three temptations in their particular social and economic contexts and reflect on our position today in the light of them.

Food

The tempter begins with focusing Jesus on what is fundamental to human well-being: food. "If you are the Son of God, command these stones to become loaves of bread" (Matthew 4:3).

Jesus is in a similar place to Israel (Exodus 16) and must learn to trust in God for what is basic: food. Jesus is tempted to renounce God and so act for his own benefit, ignoring the needs of others, including what is best for the land.[12] If Jesus does not trust God for his needs, he may disobey God's cosmic justice and exploit creation for his own gratification.

The tempter's initial challenge against Jesus seeks to seduce Jesus to satisfy his basic need for food by denying that God is the source of it. Jesus responds by affirming his commitment to God: "One does not live by bread alone, but by every word that comes from the mouth of God" (Matthew 4:4).

In this reply Jesus alludes to Israel's sojourn in the wilderness, where God supplied food to the hungry (Deuteronomy 8:3b). Jesus's words are rooted in teaching about creation in which all creation is good and belongs to God. Therefore, humanity must trust that God will provide for its needs (cf. Matthew 6:25–33).

The essence of Jesus's response is to trust in God. In not turning stones into bread, Jesus rejects values that are based on the need to exploit others for one's own benefit, but rather he trusts in God and God's faithfulness to his promises.

Ecological Significance. It is not surprising that food should be at the heart of the Devil's initial attack on Jesus. The production, distribution, and consumption of food reveal where a person's allegiances lie. Food is a human necessity, and our attitude toward food shows to what extent we trust or distrust God to provide.

Our attitude toward food also reveals the extent to which we value or do not value the rest of creation. In undermining our trust in God, the Devil entices us not only to forsake God as the one providing for our needs but even to exploit the earth's resources to get them.

Our human societies are driven by the use of violence to secure basic needs, particularly food and drink. It is easier to use brutal physical and monetary force rather than sharing with and trusting in each other. Humanity is driven by the need to seek power and control of earth's resources.

In our societies the production of food lies at the heart of our current ecological crisis (see chapter 10 for a much more extensive discussion). According to Food and Agriculture Organization, out of an estimated 860 million people who suffer from hunger in today's world, about 830 million live in the so-called developing nations.[13] This is not because they are unable to feed themselves, but, rather, because the economically powerful nations pressure poorer nations to grow for the wealthy nations. Ethiopia, a huge exporter of coffee to the developed nations, itself suffered a food crisis in 2002–2003 because coffee prices collapsed and the country had not used its own land to grow sustenance crops. Ethiopia found itself unable to feed itself.[14] We in North America and Europe expect our luxury items, but we fail to see that our need causes devastation of land and shortage of food for others. The use of land for intensive farming for coffee leads to land becoming barren,[15] as well as leaving a nation vulnerable to the vagaries of the market.

Such statistics should concern us in the light of our study of Jesus's first temptation. The society in which Jesus found himself also suffered from food shortages that arose from the control of food sources, supplies, and prices by the elite.[16] Therefore, it is very important to observe Jesus's response to political and ecological temptation as we ask ourselves about our response to the modern crisis over food, especially where we are recipients of surplus goods produced by those who have barely enough to live on.

Sensationalism

Jesus is next tempted to perform an action worthy of today's action heroes of Hollywood movies: jumping from a high building to reveal his God-given superpowers. Such an action would be sure to grab attention and get him immediate celebrity status.

Yet Jesus resists the Devil and trusts God. In his response to the Devil, Jesus provides an example for humanity of trusting in God and resisting the easy option of sensational acts.

In the second temptation, Jesus was taken from the margins of human society, the wilderness, to the center of human power, the Holy City, and placed on top of the pinnacle of the temple (Matthew 4:5). The Devil says, "If you are the Son of God, throw yourself down" (Matthew 4:6). Then the Devil quotes Scripture at Jesus: "For it is written: 'He will command his angels concerning you,' and 'On their hands they will bear you up, so that you will not dash your foot against a stone.'" (Matthew 4:6; cf. Psalm 91:11–12).

Humanity is partial to the cheap and sensational, as Roman leaders knew well. Revelation 13:13–14, for example, describes how Rome's propaganda machine was able to deceive people by performing signs and even making fire come down from heaven and images speak (Revelation 13:15).[17] Jesus's refusal to jump is an example to avoid committing sensational acts or being deceived by them (Matthew 24:23–26).

Elsewhere Jesus is tempted to take the more conventional road to success that did not involve his crucifixion. This is illustrated in the narrative where Peter tempts Jesus by telling him not to take the path to the cross (Matthew 16:13–23). Jesus responds to him by calling him "Satan" and says to him, "Get behind me." Why does Jesus say this? Peter does not favor Jesus's intentions to suffer and die on a cross, and so Peter becomes the Devil's representative, tempting Jesus away from his path. Peter wants Jesus to be a successful human leader in a way that did not mean dying on a cross.

Jesus's second temptation also anticipates his anguished words to his disciples in Gethsemane when one of them cuts off the ear of the high priest's servant; Jesus says, "Do you think that I cannot appeal to my Father, and he will at once send me more than twelve legions of angels?" (Matthew 26:53).

Jesus announces that his way is not the way of military success and mighty deeds of power. This is not his way because it is not God's way. Jesus's actual response to the Devil is: "Do not put the Lord your God to the test" (4:7). In so speaking, Jesus declares that he will not demand any display from God. Rather, he will trust God, and he will act at God's direction.

"The military way is the right way," the Devil would argue, and many devout Christians over the centuries for good political reasons have agreed. Why, then, doesn't God allow Jesus to use military force or to perform sensational acts? God's way is to transform people by calling them to repentance. Matthew is precise when he states that repentance is the message Jesus teaches after his temptations (Matthew 4:17). Only through repentance can God's creation be blessed and joyful. If Jesus performed sensational signs outside of this context, then people would follow him because of his mighty powers and not because they had repented and committed to pursuing God's cosmic justice. Sensational acts alone do not help humans to see their own sin or their involvement in perpetuating and increasing neediness, destroying other life-forms, and killing the land.

Ecological Significance. God's call to repentance lies at the center of Jesus's response to the Devil, to Peter, to the sword-carrying disciple, and to any who wish to call down fire from heaven upon their enemies. The Devil's way of using sensationalism to change things simply perpetuates an unrepentant state that is godless and harmful to creation. God's way, on the other hand, is for humans to realize they are all created and depend on God and must act accordingly.

Instead of blaming others for the ecological crisis we are in, we must look at our own lifestyles. We must not seek the sensational, jumping on easy answers to difficult questions. The ecological crisis will not be solved by sensational acts but by human repentance followed by transformed actions that respect God's creation.

Violence

In the third temptation, Jesus is enticed to become all-powerful by worshiping and serving the Devil. The Devil takes Jesus from the Holy City and places him on a mountain and reveals to him the kingdoms of the world and all their glory. The Devil tells Jesus, "All these I will give you" (Matthew 4:9). The Devil attempts to seduce Jesus with the power and wealth Rome had. For many Jews the Romans were Satan's representatives who had been responsible for the death and suffering of many Jews. Jesus rejects Satan's temptation to dominate the world using violent means, for he knew the injustices that would result from such a way. Instead, Jesus's resistance to the Devil witnessed to God's standards of justice rooted in peace.

We are told throughout the Bible that all creation belongs to God and that creation's destiny is to worship and praise God as Creator. What then is it that belongs to the Devil that he can tempt Jesus with? If all things belong to God, we must assume that the Devil is deceiving Jesus about what he is offering. In resisting the Devil's offer of the "kingdoms of the world and their splendor," Jesus exposes the Devil's offer as a lie. Jesus rejects Satan's deceiving and alluring vision of glory, saying, "Away with you, Satan! for it is written, 'Worship the Lord your God, and serve only him'" (Matthew 4:10). Jesus tells the Devil that what is needed is commitment to God and his commandments that will bring about cosmic justice.

Ecological Significance. Evil rarely confronts us in monstrous forms with horns! Rather, evil exploits our desire for what is good. Many revolutionaries have been altruistically inspired and have seized power believing things would get better once the old order was superseded. Too often, however, such persons have let their actions become manipulated by selfishness and greed.

Similarly, our modern society often tempts its citizens into dissatisfaction with what they have, selling and promoting the lie that happiness comes through possessions, despite the social and ecological costs of our acquiring more and more. Satan tempts us with dominion over such ordinary kingdoms as everyday political, social, economic, and religious life.[18]

Faced with this temptation, like Jesus, we too must confess our faith, worshiping and serving God by practicing cosmic justice.

Chapter Summary

Jesus learned about God and about his own call through a combination of experiencing life alone in the wilderness and thinking about Scripture, particularly Scripture's narration of Israel's time in the desert and Isaiah's wonderfully pictorial vision of a completed creation where cosmic justice would reign. Jesus in the wilderness succeeded where Israel had failed, exemplifying in his responses to the Devil a love for and trust in God and a commitment to cosmic justice rather than exploitation, sensationalism, and violence. We need to repent and follow Jesus's example, looking toward a new creation on earth where

> the wolf shall live with the lamb, the leopard shall lie down with the kid, the calf and the lion and the fatling together, and a little child shall lead them. The cow and the bear shall graze, their young shall lie down together; and the lion shall eat straw like the ox. The nursing child shall play over the hole of the asp, and the weaned child shall put its hand on the adder's den. (Isaiah 11:6–8)

Reflection Questions

1. What difference does it make to begin a discussion about caring for the earth from the perspective of Jesus's time in the wilderness?
2. What temptations do you think you would have if you were isolated in a desert without the normal physical comforts?
3. In what ways do you face temptations similar to the ones Jesus faced?

Chapter 4

JESUS "WITH THE WILD BEASTS"
(MARK 1:13)

Thomas Berry writes:

> We misconceive our role if we consider that our historical mission is to "civilize" or to "domesticate" the planet, as though wildness is something destructive rather than the ultimate creative modality of any form of earthly being. We are not here to control. We are here to become integral with the larger Earth community.[1]

Thomas Berry's words are apt for beginning our study of Mark 1:13, which tells us that Jesus "was in the wilderness forty days, tempted by Satan; and he was with the wild beasts."

Mark's description of Jesus being "with the wild animals" (NIV) might lead to a vision of Jesus as "a beast tamer," but such a view is inconsistent with the broader biblical story. In this chapter I will focus on the phrase "with the wild animals" (NIV) as presenting an Edenic state that involves harmony with all creation.

Human-Centeredness and the Creation Mandate

Yann Arthus-Bertrand perceptively observes in *A Hymn to the Planet and Humanity*:

> Thanks to our mastery of the world, we have a tendency to relate everything back to ourselves and to evaluate everything on a human scale—that of the few decades of our individual lives, or the few thousand or million square miles of the country we inhabit. But will we ever learn to take care of the planet we inhabit, of its limited and precious resources, so that we can hand it on in good condition to our descendants?[2]

Arthus-Bertrand points to the human-centeredness of the human race but at the same time asks whether we are up to the task of doing what God commands us to do, that is, to take care of the planet we inhabit.

Human-Centeredness and Its Consequences

Humanity's failure to see itself as part of a wider and complex ecosystem has dire consequences for our planet today. Oil production and transportation, for example, disrupt human populations, as well as the animal and fish life of oil-producing regions. The social and environmental costs of oil production are extensive. As well as the destruction of wildlife and biodiversity, there are increasing loss of fertile soil, pollution of the air, and decreasing access to drinking water.[3] So why do we continue to go to such lengths to get oil? Because humanity sees itself as master of all creation, with the right to dominate and exploit it.

We build hyrdroelectric dams without really considering the effects of impeding the flow of over half of the planet's major rivers, preventing migrations, and permanently affecting living conditions for many species. Similarly, we fail to see that we imprison living creatures on one side or the other of insurmountable barriers because of our need for roads and highways.[4] Human-centeredness leads to a manipulation of nature. We hunt animals not to satisfy hunger but to provide luxury items that spell extinction in some cases. Other examples of manipulation include using animals for entertainment, such as bullfights or dogfights.

Within the Bible there is a vision of peace with the wild animals. Because of our human-centeredness, however, we have not devoted ourselves to absorbing this vision and have conveniently sidestepped its implications to our way of life. I believe this is due to the inability of humanity to perceive creation as God's good work and ourselves as "created." If all creation is God's good gift, we should treat it with care and compassion, but human-centeredness too often prevents us from understanding or doing this.

The Creation Mandate of Genesis

Human-centeredness is evident in the way we have misinterpreted the Genesis creation narratives throughout history, believing that being made in the image of God (Genesis 1:26–28) is a mandate to violate and dominate all creation and ignoring the wider canon of Scripture in which God is one who cares. Robert Murray observes rightly in some detail that having dominion and subduing in Genesis 1:28 are too crudely translated in terms of exploitation.[5] Christopher Wright comments: "It seems clear that God here passes on to human hands a delegated form of God's own kingly authority over the whole of his creation,"[6] and this means caring for that creation. The wider biblical testimony tells us that God is Creator, preserver, carer, and shepherd. His work exudes wisdom in planning, power in execution, and goodness in completion (see Psalm 145). Being made in the likeness of God does not elevate humanity in a tyrannical way but rather gives humans responsibility to relate with fellow sisters and brothers, as well as with the rest of creation, in a close, intimate, caring way.

In Genesis 2:15 humanity is told to till and care for the garden of Eden. The words "till" and "care" are closely connected to the word "serve" in Hebrew. Such actions are in contrast to actions of controlling and violating. Jeremiah, for example, condemns the inhabitants of the earth for saying, "I will not serve [care]." The refusal to serve is disobedience to God (Jeremiah 2:20a).

Jewish Hope for Harmony with Animals

There is agreement among many scholars that Mark 1:13 shows that God envisions a harmony throughout creation, where the wilderness instead of being a place to fear and tame is one that is the theater of God's glory. I follow the line of interpretation that believes that Mark portrays Jesus in peaceable companionship with animals, which were habitually perceived as inimical and threatening to humans.[7] To support this interpretation of Mark 1:13 we must consider how "wild beasts" would be understood within an early Jewish context.

In the Old Testament, wild and dangerous animals are often associated with the desert and wilderness (Isaiah 13:21–22; 34:13–15; Psalm 22:12–21). Such animals are often used as symbols of Israel's enemies (Ezekiel 34:5, 8; Daniel 7:1–8). Wild beasts in the wilderness are seen also as demons (Isaiah 13:21–22; 34:13–15), which leads to a connection between a future hope of defeating demons and a subjection of wild beasts.

Such a negative perception of wild animals is more a consequence of the fall than something God originally intended, however. God had established human dominion over the animals (Genesis 1:26, 28; Psalm 8:6–8), which should have been peaceful and harmonious but became distorted by violence.

Even in the Old Testament's post-fall state, however, it was still thought that a righteous person could enjoy the relationship to animals that God originally intended for humanity (Job 5:22–23). Hosea, for example, looked for a time of peace and harmony between wild animals and people (2:18). The classical expression of hope for peace between humans and wild animals is Isaiah 11:6–9 (cf. 65:17).

Jesus's Friendship with the Wild Beasts

There is no suggestion in the Greek of Mark 1:13 that the wild beasts were at one with Satan in tempting Jesus as is sometimes argued. Between the known enemy of God, Satan, and the known friends of God, the angels, the animals may seem to be in an ambiguous situation here. But we know from the Old Testament material above that there was a strong expectation of harmony between a righteous person and the wild animals in God's re-created world. In the book of Job there is such a hope of harmony: "For you shall be in league with the stones of the field, and the wild animals shall be at peace with you" (Job 5:23).

Despite the fear of wild animals, then, Jewish eschatological hope in God's re-creating actions was rooted in a vision of human harmony with all creation. This vision insists that enmity between humans and wild animals will be healed. The emphasis in Jewish eschatological hope is on peaceable relationships (Job 5:23) rather than human dominion over the animals.[8] It is this peace with wild animals that Jesus exemplifies in Mark 1:13.

Ecological Application of Mark 1:13

Jesus's being "with the wild beasts" provides a notable countercultural witness to cultures that perceive animals and the rest of creation as existing only to satisfy human needs. If God's concern is orientated only toward humanity, then why would Jesus begin his ministry in the wilderness far from humanity? Rather, God's re-creating work involves the wilderness and everything it represents—everything that is not human, as well as what is human. God is not concerned only for humanity; God is cosmos centered, concerned with humans, as well as the rest of creation, and we massively misunderstand Jesus and Christianity if we don't sensitize and devote ourselves to this God of all creation.

How can we emulate Jesus's peaceful relations with the wild animals? A report to the World Council of Churches, as part of its "Justice, Peace and the Integrity of Creation" program, encourages members of the Christian community to respond to the following:[9]

- Avoid cosmetics and household products that have been cruelly tested on animals. Instead buy cruelty-free items.
- Avoid clothing and other aspects of fashion that have a history of cruelty to animals, products of the fur industry in particular. Instead purchase clothes that are "cruelty-free."

- Avoid meat and animal products that have been produced on factory farms. Instead purchase meat and animal products from sources where the animals have been treated with respect, or abstain from these products altogether.
- Avoid patronizing forms of entertainment that treat animals as means to human ends. Instead, seek benign forms of entertainment, ones that nurture a sense of wonder of God's creation and reawaken that duty of conviviality that we can discharge by living respectfully in community with all life, the animals included.

Chapter Summary

In this chapter we have considered Jesus's being "with the wild beasts" in the context of God's vision for Israel, humanity, and all creation. In Mark 1:13 we catch a glimpse of that vision where Jesus neither terrorizes nor dominates the wild animals; he does not domesticate or even make pets of them. He is simply with them. Jesus's companionable presence with the wild animals affirms their independent value for themselves and for God. He does not adopt them into the human world but leaves them in their wilderness, affirming them as creatures that share the world with us in the community of God's creation.[10]

In our present time living in the hope of God's future cosmic justice, not yet realized, it is our privilege and responsibility to be caught up in God's vision of cosmic justice, acting according to our gifts to care for all that God has entrusted to us, including other living creatures.

Reflection Questions

1. Have your attitudes toward animals been challenged by Mark 1:13?
2. What can you do to encourage greater harmony with the wild creatures where you live?
3. Does the way you eat fit with God's vision of cosmic justice for wild creatures?

Chapter 5

BAD NEWS

"The Spirit of the Lord is upon me, because he has anointed me to bring good news to the [afflicted]. He has sent me to proclaim release to the captives and recovery of sight to the blind, to let the oppressed go free, to proclaim the year of the Lord's favor" (Luke 4:18–19).

Echlin observes that Luke 4:18–19 is one of the richest ecological texts in the New Testament.[1] This may seem, at first, a surprising claim to make as Luke 4:18–19 appears to relate only to humans. So why is it ecologically relevant? It is ecologically significant because Jesus's teaching about social justice includes ecological justice. Liberation and healing for afflicted and disempowered humans must correspond to the treatment of the rest of creation.

I have titled this chapter "Bad News" because Jesus's above words are initially "bad news" to most of us in the West who put our trust too heavily in material wealth for security and well-being. In this chapter we will see that Jesus challenges "those who have" to trust God to care for their needs by sharing what they have with those who don't have.

Luke 4:18: Jesus and Generosity

Luke speaks of good news for the "afflicted" in 4:18. "Afflicted" occurs elsewhere in Luke, and on every occasion it refers to the materially poor in contrast to those who are better off (6:20; 7:22; 14:13, 21; 16:19–20, 22–23; 18:22; 19:8; and 21:3). John Nolland writes, "To be poor, hungry, and weeping is not at all the situation that Luke envisages in the ideal state of Christian existence (Acts 2:43–47; 4:4)."[2] Poverty is not idealized in Luke, but the reversal of it is called for (Luke 1:48, 52–53; 16:25). This is evidenced in early Christian lifestyle choices that resulted in none being needy among the fellowship of the early church because generosity prevailed (Acts 4:34).

"Good News" and Jubilee

Luke 4:18–19 alludes to the sabbatical year of Jubilee when the afflicted will be shown generosity, when all slaves are freed, debts canceled, the blind see, and prisoners are released.[3] The Jubilee laws are an example of cosmic justice. The Jubilee good news Jesus speaks of in Luke 4:19 is the "year of the Lord's favor" and is an allusion to Isaiah 61:2 in which God promises to show his favor to the afflicted through Jubilee generosity.[4] The good news of Isaiah 61:1–2 meant the restoration of land and livelihood to the afflicted—bad news to those who had plenty unless they embraced the message and shared material wealth. Isaiah 61:1–2 looks to the time when God's reign will be complete and when "cosmic justice" reigns.

In the Promised Land there were to be no poor because God had blessed the people who came out of their poverty and oppression in Egypt (Deuteronomy 15:4). However, in Deuteronomy 15:11, it is assumed there will be poor. Why is this? Christopher Wright comments that because of endemic greed and violence, poverty results. Deuteronomy expresses a realistic view that in the here and now there will be poverty, but in the future when God's will is done on earth and in heaven, everyone will have what is necessary (Micah 4:4; cf. Isaiah 2:1–5).[5]

To proclaim good news to the afflicted in Luke 4:18 should be read as an encompassing designation of Jesus's whole ministry, which is expanded upon in the remainder of verse 18. As long as there are oppressed, hungry, naked, and sick people, Christians cannot rest easily.

Jesus's calling as the Anointed One was to heal and free the afflicted (Luke 7:22), and this defines the mission for Christians then and today.

Sharing Wealth

The good news Jesus brings involves the transformation of those in society who benefit from the affliction of others. Initially this is "bad news" to those who have wealth because it means relinquishing control of it, which is not easy. An example of how hard it is to do this can be observed in the reluctance of Ananias and his wife, Sapphira, to give all their wealth to the church (Acts 5:1–11). The Gospels also speak of a rich man who was sad on hearing Jesus tell him he must sell everything and give to the poor (Luke 18:22–24).

We should be vigilant against explaining away difficult words of Jesus that unsettle us. Those of us, for example, who are materially comfortable should be on our guard against spiritualizing the "afflicted" so that we ourselves can fit into this "afflicted" category. Often "afflicted" is taken to mean "humble,"[6] an interpretation I am dubious of. This incorrect understanding allows us to envisage becoming "humble" without the struggle of letting go of our material treasures.

Jesus, in contrast, calls for generous sharing as a form of counter-cultural witness to the human urge to compete, acquire, and consume. Jesus was not alone in believing in the importance of generosity. In Psalm 112 the person who loves God has wealth (v. 3), but takes pity and lends (v. 5) and is open-handed in giving to the poor (v. 9). Such is what Jesus expects from those who have wealth.

In seeking to alleviate the suffering of the afflicted, we must work to configure new ways of caring that remove material affliction and prevent the desecration of the rest of creation. Initially this is bad news to our present world order based on the canons of economic growth. But those of us who are materially fortunate must first accept the "bad news" of our need to share before we can realize fully the wonder of the good news. If Christians wish to share in the good news with the afflicted, then it is necessary that they commit themselves to sharing what they have in excess so that they can rejoice with God at the health of all his creation. This does not mean that Christians embrace material poverty, but that all should have enough and that poverty should no longer exist.

Rejection of Jesus

Jesus's good news is rejected by some of those in the synagogue. Why was Jesus driven out of the synagogue? What did he say to cause an outcry against him? We can understand more of Jesus's good news message when we consider why his message was so contrary to the hopes of Galilean listeners.

As we have seen, the "afflicted" Jesus refers to did not include people who had a reasonably secure means of supporting themselves.[7] Yet many in the synagogue, including Pharisees and the normal mass of Jewish people, saw themselves as the "poor of God" or the "afflicted" because they were oppressed by foreigners. Jesus upset significant notaries in the synagogue when he challenged their perception of themselves as "afflicted." Jesus's editing of Isaiah 61:1–2 helps us understand why his audience was offended. His significant omission of "the day of vengeance of our God" from Isaiah 61 is a clue to what triggers the synagogue's rejection of him. Isaiah 61 was understood by Jews in a very nationalist sense, particularly verses 6–7. They desired that Judea and Galilee be cleansed of the oppressing Roman force that imposed high taxes, controlled the use of land, and flaunted its power through its powerful army, buildings, ceremonies, and defiling of sacred spaces.[8] Jesus omits the vengeful verses of Isaiah that the crowd would have rejoiced in most and with which it was familiar. The Aramaic version of Isaiah reflects a synagogue interpretive tradition with which Jesus's audience would have been familiar: "You shall eat the possession of the Gentiles, and in their glory you shall be indulged. Instead of your being ashamed and confounded, two for one the benefits I promise you I will bring to you, and the Gentiles will be ashamed who were boasting in their lot."[9] This early Aramaic tradition reveals the understandable hatred of the oppressed for the oppressor. Jesus's editing of Isaiah 61 is thus clearly intentional and notable for its absence of nationalism and pride.

In challenging the synagogue's desire for vengeance, Jesus also drew upon stories about Elijah and Elisha. Jesus reminds the crowd that during a famine, Elijah didn't help Israelite widows but rather helped the widow at Zarephath in Sidon in Syria. He was not interested in Israelites but was more concerned with a poor Gentile widow. In the same vein Jesus provocatively recalls how Elisha cured a leper who was a military officer in the Syrian army yet did not go to the lepers of Israel. The "afflicted" for Elisha were not lepers in Israel but a leprous high-ranking army officer in Syria. Luke tells us the response of the crowd: "When they heard this, all in the synagogue were filled with rage" (Luke 4:28). Such a response is easily understandable for anyone who has felt persecuted by Gentiles. The very identity of the people of Israel was defined by its desire to be separated from Gentiles. Jesus challenged this.

Jesus goes to the afflicted in Israel. However, he makes the point that to be afflicted means to be truly poor and not merely to have Gentiles dictating one's affairs. In Luke 4, Jesus was reminding some in the synagogue that their responsibilities were not to extort and cause further suffering to the truly afflicted. In fact, elsewhere Jesus condemns people for putting burdens on the afflicted and not helping them (Luke 11:46) and for killing those who seek justice (Luke 11:47–51).

Jesus challenged his audience to think more deeply about the truly "afflicted" and so consider their own responsibility for the existence of real affliction in their own land. He encouraged his synagogue audience to rethink the laws of Jubilee. As long as there were afflicted in the land, the land was falling short of God's standards of righteousness and his commandments were being disobeyed. Jesus was telling them to stop feeling sorry for themselves and do something about the truly poor. The fact that Jesus proclaims good news to the poor is testimony of how far short those in the synagogue were of keeping and practicing God's commandments of generosity as specified in the Jubilee laws.

Importance of Generosity

Let's consider other gospel texts that teach the importance of generosity for Christians.

The Parable of the Barn (Luke 12:13–21)

Jesus criticizes a rich landowner for hoarding his goods and saying to himself: "You have ample goods laid up for many years; relax, eat, drink, be merry" (Luke 12:19). Jesus states that such a man is a fool, for his life has been based on the wrong principle of caring only for himself.

The rich man failed to recognize that he was accountable to God for all he owned.[10] He had no more right to the land and its fruits than any other person. The rich man showed no awareness that the bumper crop that had led to his good fortune had been a gift from God. He saw it as his crop. The rich man did not realize that the bellies of the poor were much safer storerooms than his barns.[11] This parable is a good example of Jesus's teaching that challenges the motto "Charity begins at home." I am puzzled every time I read this parable how Christianity came to be identified with making money and becoming prosperous.

For a wealthy person this parable would be bad news, but not because the landowner has pulled down a small barn and built bigger barns to store his bumper harvest; it is bad news because he kept it for himself, so rejecting God's mandate to share.

In sum, this parable is bad news to those whose joy rests in their material wealth. Jesus tells his audience that those who store up treasures for themselves are not rich towards God (Luke 12:21). Jesus doesn't criticize wealth, but he attacks those who keep it for themselves. Jesus teaches about the importance of generosity and the foolishness of hoarding.

Zacchaeus (Luke 19:1–10)

Jesus never rejected the rich, but he called them to repent so that they might experience God's pain at the injustices done to his beautiful creation. Jesus demanded a real political and economic response. Surely this was bad news to people like Zacchaeus who would be confronted by their ill-gotten gains.

Zacchaeus was a head tax collector. Further, he was a representative of the hated Roman colonial forces and therefore a social pariah to many Jews. His wealth was gained from his oppression of the afflicted. Yet Jesus accepts him. His surprising act of eating with Zacchaeus resulted in Zacchaeus's repentance exemplified in his generosity to those he had harmed (Luke 19:1–10).

Through eating with Jesus, Zacchaeus came to recognize that his wealth had been accumulated by violence against the afflicted. In repenting he accepts the bad news that he must give away what he has acquired through violence, so he can know the good news of liberation. He could only act generously because he saw the frightening truth that he had not only cheated others but had robbed God of what was his alone. Zacchaeus experienced through Jesus God's concern for the afflicted.

We must also acknowledge that Zacchaeus's repentance is good news to all those who lacked basic necessities. He is no longer their oppressor but one who will proclaim good news and bring about healing by enabling the poor to share the earth's resources.

Finally, we should consider that Zacchaeus in giving away more than he owes shows his trust in God. We must assume that Zacchaeus's repentance and consequent generosity will mean he loses his job or that he will need to resign. He will lose his own livelihood, and he will become a vulnerable person dependent on the generosity of others, perhaps those he had repaid.

The Centurion (Luke 7:1–10)

Jesus says that a Gentile centurion who asks him for help has great faith because he trusts in Jesus's ability to heal a slave whom the centurion loves (Luke 7:9). The centurion was in no way economically poor, and he could afford the best physicians, but despite his own power and wealth, he trusted God instead.

The centurion is described as one who cared for the exiled people of Israel by loving them and building a synagogue for them (7:5). His concern for the afflicted servant was clearly important to Jesus and praised as such. Jesus contrasts the Gentile's faith with the lack of faith of rich and privileged Jews in Israel. Unlike his commendation of the Gentile centurion, Jesus condemns the Jewish leaders for neglecting justice (11:42), for seeking the approval of people (11:43), and for devouring widows' houses (20:47). The centurion in contrast is depicted as perceptive, trusting, and generous.

Jesus's Disciples

Jesus's disciples are not from among the afflicted. James and John, for example, share a fishing business with their father and have hired workers (Mark 1:20). Another one of the disciples was a tax collector (Mark 2:14) who gave up this lucrative life for the way of a nomadic teacher (Matthew 8:18–21). Jesus elsewhere instructs his twelve disciples that whenever they go on their mission they must take nothing with them, suggesting that they had goods that they could have taken. Indeed, Peter and probably all the disciples asked in effect on numerous occasions: "What will I get in return for what I have done?" (Luke 18:28–30). They had given up much to follow Jesus, so much that Peter questions Jesus about their future rewards.

Yet the disciples, like Zacchaeus, learned that the wealth and property they had were not sufficient for their lives. As seekers of truth they realized that they must embrace a way of life devoted to imitating Jesus's nomadic way, caring for the afflicted.

Luke 4:18 and a Vision of Harmony

We have seen that the Bible can be summed up in three words: creation, fall, and re-creation. At the heart of the Old Testament is the hope of God's completion of his creation. This hope on many occasion fuels the imagination of some of the Old Testament writers in which they present beautiful visions of environmental harmony. Such, also, energized the minds of the New Testament writers. It is important that we now devote some time to understanding Luke 4:18 alongside such visions.

Luke 4:18, Isaiah 11, and Isaiah 35

N. T. Wright and Echlin both observe that Luke 4:18–19 is an echo of Isaiah 11:1–10 with its vision of cosmic justice for the afflicted and where the lion will eat straw (11:7).[12] Isaiah sees good news for the poor involving peace and harmony throughout nature. While the connection between the texts is not obvious, it seems highly likely that Jesus's good news was in line with Isaiah 11. Jesus is an anointed figure like the figure in Isaiah 11:2. Like the figure of Isaiah 11, Jesus teaches that he too will bring about God's will.

A more obvious link is between Luke 4:18 and Isaiah 35. Both Isaiah 35 and Luke 4:18–19 mention that the healing of the blind will take place. Isaiah 35 also adds an ecological healing that echoes Isaiah 11:1–10.

To this extent we must see the good news Jesus speaks of in Luke 4:18–19 alongside both Isaiah 11 and 35. These texts tell us something of Jesus's understanding of his work and teachings. Throughout Jesus's healing ministry he opened the eyes of the blind, cured the deaf, made the lame walk and the mute talk, and raised the dead (Luke 7:22), healing deeds Isaiah 35 expected of an anointed figure.

But is there any evidence that Jesus performed ecological healings that correspond with the harmony visions of Isaiah 11 and 35?

Jesus's Calming of the Storm (Mark 4:35–41)

The biggest obstacle to seeing the connection between social and environmental concerns in the New Testament is the lack of evidence in Jesus's ministry of healing nature. I want to consider one piece of evidence that shows Jesus's concern for nature.

Mark states that Jesus rebukes the wind and said to the sea, "Peace! Be still!" (Mark 4:39). Jesus's calming of the storm anticipates God's final elimination of chaos from the natural world and the dawning of the kingdom of God hoped for in Isaiah 11:1–10; 35; and 61.

Bauckham comments that "the nature miracles show that the healing of the human relationship with nonhuman nature belongs to the holistic salvation that the kingdom of God means in the Gospels."[13] Echlin adds that "the calming story connotes the expulsion of evil, the healing of nature, and includes water—in a word, salvation ecology and salvation history."[14] Jesus's calming of the storm is a vision of peace and harmony with all creation. The storm in which the disciples find themselves is seen as needing to be constantly restrained by God. Jesus's words used to calm the storm allude to the Old Testament where God subdues the waters of chaos (Psalm 104:7; Job 26:12). Bauckham rightly believes that the Gospels are inviting us to see the calming as anticipating God's final elimination of chaos from the natural world. It is a sign of Jesus's inauguration of the kingdom of God.[15]

Christopher Wright comments that if Isaiah 35 describes the completion of creation to which we should look, we must ask what we should be doing to bring this about.[16] We must learn from what Israel is expected to do. Israel is ordered to obey God's Jubilee with its emphasis on resting the land (Leviticus 25:4), freeing slaves (Leviticus 25:10), restoring land and property to those who have been dispossessed (Leviticus 25:13), and caring for the dispossessed (Leviticus 25:35). Living according to God's commandments is living in harmony with creation, resulting in the land being healthy and fruitful (see chapter 2).

Ecological Significance

We must not be inclined to define the poor as being the spiritually humble and meek. Such a reading empties Jesus's teaching of its radical concern for pain and suffering to the materially poor brought about by the rich. Robert White poses well the ecological significance of Luke 4:18–19:

> Those who live in high-income nations including Europe, North America and Australia, with high standards of living

achieved partly through the selfish and unsustainable use of natural resources, have a particular responsibility to care for others affected by global climate change. . . . Christians should care for our unborn successors and for the strangers and the foreigner (Leviticus 19:33–34; Jeremiah 22:3; Matthew 25:35–45) even if they live out of sight on the other side of the world but are affected by our actions.[17]

The ecological crisis is caused partly by nations, peoples, and individuals living as though they had a right to surplus foods and goods, while the producers often struggle on what is far below the breadline. North America and Europe's taste for the exotic puts huge demands on poor nations. McDonagh puts it well:

> It is hard to visualize that a meal in one's favourite fast-food restaurant damages the tropical forest. Yet it most surely does. The conversion of tropical rain forest to cattle ranches to supply the fast-food hamburger industry of First World countries is the most wasteful and destructive use of the tropical rain forest. The land is normally cleared through burning the cover. The soil is quickly degraded as erosion is speeded up by the constant pressure of cattle hooves on the fragile soil. When the land becomes exhausted, the ranchers move on to repeat the cycle of destruction.[18]

Loss of forest means the loss of a way of life for the indigenous peoples. Winner of the Nobel Peace Prize, Kenyan environmentalist Wangari Maathai, in her autobiography, *Unbowed: One Woman's Story*, describes her return to her rural home where she had known plenty:

> When I went home to visit my family in Nyeri, I had another indication of the changes under way around us. I saw rivers silted with topsoil, much of which was coming from the forests where plantations of commercial trees had replaced indigenous forest. I noticed that much of the land that had been covered by trees, bushes, and grasses when I was growing up had been replaced by tea and coffee.[19]

Western addiction to coffee leads to the loss of land for others who produce this crop at the expense of growing food for their local community. Maathai again comments on research that

> found that children in the central region of Kenya were suffering from diseases associated with malnutrition. This was an eye-opener for me, since that is where I come from and knew from personal experience that the central region was one of the most fertile in Kenya. But times had changed. Many farmers had converted practically all of their land into growing coffee and tea to sell in the international market. These "cash crops" were occupying land previously used to produce food for people to eat.[20]

Further, it is observed that the famines that have become characteristic of parts of sub-Saharan Africa are a consequence of agricultural abuse of the land by colonial and postcolonial landowners looking for quick returns from cash crops that are unsuitable for the cleared bush and forest land.[21] However, we in the West too easily blame famine on laziness or corruption. This is not true. Amartya Sen, who won the Nobel Prize in economics for his studies on the economics of famines, comments that famines are not caused by lack of food, but lack of rights.[22] Before the advent of European farms and plantations, Africans were not malnourished, and their lands were not eroded and drought prone but were well developed and abundant.[23] It is when a country loses sovereignty over its own food that problems occur.

Malawi, for example, was pressured by the World Bank as well as European and US agencies to export for the Western market. Instead of begging for food after a famine, Malawi's government started plans for food self-reliance and put money into projects to help people grow their own food. Wayne Roberts concludes, "The success of the Malawi project confirms the need to recognize a principle of food sovereignty—local reliance and self-rule in food matters—rather than placing authority in institutions and markets far from the scene."[24]

Chapter Summary

This chapter has been about good news and bad news. It is good news for the afflicted when the wealthy repent of their personal, social, and ecological sins. Jesus's disciples are to repent and to proclaim God's concern for the afflicted in our world so that the earth's resources may be distributed in the way that God intended. It seems highly likely that Jesus is demanding an implementation of Jubilee requirements, which means those who have must distribute fairly.[25] Jesus is calling his followers to trust in God and practice the laws of Jubilee. Luke 4:18–19 calls disciples to work against poverty, hunger, and misery. They are to be committed to a lifestyle of sharing,[26] simplicity,[27] material dependence,[28] and constant vigilance against the "deceitfulness of riches."[29]

Good news to the afflicted is also good news for the land and all the rest of creation. Land is not given for the purposes of the rich oppressing the poor. Land is important to God and is meant to be fertile and teeming with life. When the earth is truly valued by people as God's gift, people will see it as a living being and treat it with care. The land feeds and sustains people, but when people use it for power and control, then they will treat it with disrespect, and it will die.

Reflection Questions

1. How should we react to those who tell us that we have too much and that we are not as generous and kind as we think we are?
2. How would Jesus regard calls to cancel the debts of poorer nations?
3. How can you put into practice Jesus's good news to the poor?

Chapter 6

THE BEATITUDES 1: MATTHEW 5:36

Frederick Bruner comments that the Beatitudes recorded in Matthew 5:3–12 "are the most significant words ever spoken; their simplicity is deceptive. There is gold under the ground."[1] I devote the next two chapters to Jesus's Beatitudes to learn what they might tell us about being Christian in a world that, more than at any time in human history, is causing permanent harm to all creation.

It is vital that we assess carefully the identity of those being "blessed" in the Beatitudes and the nature of their being "blessed." Misunderstanding can result in emptying Jesus's teachings of their original meaning, particularly tempting when this meaning challenges those who own much.

I am persuaded by Warren Carter's initial insight that "the poor in spirit" in the first beatitude are the economically poor whose spirits are being crushed by economic injustice. They are those who have no hope because of the corrosive effect of hopeless material poverty.[2] I will argue that the first four beatitudes all refer to those crying out in pain and suffering.

Structure of the Beatitudes

Verses 3–12 consist of nine beatitudes. The nine beatitudes are divided into three sections:

Verses 3–6—Four beatitudes that refer to the downcast
Blessed are the poor in spirit, for theirs is the kingdom of heaven.
Blessed are those who mourn, for they will be comforted.
Blessed are the meek, for they will inherit the earth.
Blessed are those who hunger and thirst for righteousness, for they will be filled.

Verses 7–10—Four beatitudes that refer to those who must act on behalf of the downcast
Blessed are the merciful, for they will receive mercy.
Blessed are the pure in heart, for they will see God.
Blessed are the peacemakers, for they will be called children of God.
Blessed are those who are persecuted for righteousness' sake, for theirs is the kingdom of heaven.

Verses 11–12—One beatitude directed to the disciples
Blessed are you when people revile you and persecute you and utter all kinds of evil against you falsely on my account. Rejoice and be glad, for your reward is great in heaven, for in the same way they persecuted the prophets who were before you.

The first set of four beatitudes refers to the powerless victims of our world whose hopelessness is increased by worldviews that perpetuate and increase the gap between rich and poor. The second set of four beatitudes present the kingdom values necessary to remove the gap between rich and poor. Finally, the last summarizing beatitude is specifically directed to Jesus's disciples.

The first two sets of beatitudes are linked by the phrase "kingdom of heaven," which acts as brackets enclosing the eight beatitudes (vv. 3 and 10). It may also be significant that the first four beatitudes are concerned with themes related through the Greek letter "*p*" (pi): *ptōchon* (afflicted), *penthountes* (those who weep), *praeis* (the oppressed/meek), and *peinontes* (those who hunger).

Literary Context

The Beatitudes are Jesus's first words of teaching in Matthew's gospel. The scene is Jesus sitting on top of a mountain to teach his disciples. We discover from Matthew 4:18–22 that there are at least four disciples present: Peter, Andrew, James, and John. Some of the other disciples may also have been there, but not the tax collector whose call is only narrated in 9:9. These four disciples were fishermen whom Jesus called from their work (4:18–22). It is a picture of ordinary, hardworking Jewish men having a special audience with Jesus. We must not think of them as afflicted with diseases, poverty, or hunger.

Matthew sums up Jesus's ministry in 4:23–24: Jesus taught and proclaimed the good news of the kingdom throughout Galilee, a ministry that is corroborated throughout Matthew's gospel. The Beatitudes summarize Jesus's teaching, which is recorded further in Matthew 5–7. His "dawning kingdom" preaching is then demonstrated by healing acts that are evidenced in nine miracles of healing in Matthew 8–9.

Just as in Luke 4, which we considered in the previous chapter, Matthew here presents Jesus as one who announces good news to the afflicted and brings sight to the blind and freedom to the oppressed.

What does "Blessed" mean?

Only the most naive or heartless can claim that those who cry out for the basic necessities of life are joyful in their affliction. "Joyful" to the afflicted can only mean the "joyfulness" of one whose destitute situation is being reversed; it is the "joyfulness" of an innocent man or woman in prison being told he or she is to be freed.

In the Beatitudes, Jesus is not romanticizing poverty by calling his followers to embrace it. He challenges those who "have" to see to it that they share what they have. The good news of God's kingdom brings release and healing to all who are afflicted in creation, even the mourning land and wild animals (Hosea 4:3). Those who experience Jesus's healing hand and voice will cry out in joyfulness like the prophet Isaiah:

> How beautiful upon the mountains are the feet of the messenger who announces peace, who brings good news, who announces salvation, who says to Zion, "Your God reigns." (Isaiah 52:7)[3]

God's reign is revealed in Jesus's preaching, teaching, exorcisms, and healings. Jesus's work brings present joy to the afflicted. Matthew writes, "Jesus went throughout Galilee, teaching in their synagogues and proclaiming the good news of the kingdom and curing every disease and every sickness among the people" (Matthew 4:23). The poor and afflicted are the beneficiaries of God's concern, and that is why they are joyful. This is not some otherworldly hope. It is the hope of cosmic justice on earth in material form.

Further, being "blessed" is also used in the sense of "joyful is a person who is in the business of doing God's work," which is appropriate to the second set of four beatitudes. Jesus teaches, "Blessed is that slave whom his master will find at work when he arrives" (Matthew 24:46). This servant is blessed because he or she has faithfully carried out his or her master's instructions to provide adequate food and drink and to care for the general welfare of the master's subjects. I will argue in the next chapter that such joyfulness of those who are more privileged is related precisely to bringing "joy" to the afflicted mentioned in 5:3–6.

Matthew 5:3–6

The first four beatitudes begin with God's favored people: widows, orphans, refugees, the poor, any who are marginalized and victims of society. For Matthew's Jesus, this is primarily humanity, but I would not presume to impose a modern human-centered view on Jesus and his contemporaries. There is a strong link between human poverty and ecological poverty. Concern for human poverty is surely the beginning of concern for the environment.

The existence of poverty among our own species is an offense, and putting this right is essential. None can claim to be "blessed" when they see the faces and hear the cries of the afflicted. The poor and afflicted can be "blessed" only when their affliction is removed. For the wealthy, being "blessed" means faithfulness to God's command to share with the poor. God releases the oppressed, so the formerly oppressed are to treat others compassionately (see also Matthew 18:23–35).

When Jesus calls the afflicted and humiliated "blessed" in verses 3–6, he is critiquing human societies that create and allow such poverty and suffering. I think also it is possible that Jesus had in mind the very groaning of creation when he blesses the poor. These very verses should shock our consciences just as they did Matthew's original readers. Jesus appears in the traditions of the Old Testament prophets and psalmists as reprimanding the wealthy and comfortable for not showing compassion to the oppressed as God had demonstrated to Israel in Egypt. In sum, the existence of poverty is an indictment against our comfortable lifestyles.

Beatitude One

> Blessed are the poor in spirit, for theirs is the kingdom of heaven.

The phrase "blessed are the poor in spirit" is often paraphrased "joyful are those who know they are small and insignificant before God." This interpretation is a little too convenient for those living materially comfortable lives because it allows them to imagine that Jesus is referring to them. Because they confess God as Creator, they think themselves humble before God and therefore "poor in spirit." Jesus, however, teaches that it is the really powerless who are to be blessed in the arrival of God's reign in Jesus. We must not spiritualize verse 3, for in doing so we divest God of his special concern for the afflicted as revealed in Scripture.

In view of the tendency to spiritualize poverty, I will argue in more detail regarding the identity of the poor. The word "poor" that we find in Matthew 5:3 is a very specific Greek word, *ptōchos*, meaning materially needy. It is unlikely that Matthew uses the word with spiritual associations because elsewhere he shows himself familiar with vocabulary more appropriate for describing humility and meekness. For example, in Matthew, Jesus describes himself as meek and humble (Greek: *tapeinos*) in heart (11:29).

My argument is further supported when we observe the uses of *ptōchos* elsewhere in Matthew. "Poor" (*ptōchos*) occurs three other times, without "in spirit." In 11:4–5 Jesus refers to his good news to the "poor" as a sign of his being the anointed figure of Isaiah 61:1 (cf. Luke 7:22). Here "poor" clearly refers to afflicted groups and individuals, as in Matthew 4:23: those with diseases and the sick.

In Matthew 19:21 Jesus tells a rich man that if he wishes to have treasure in heaven he must sell his possessions and give to the poor. In Matthew 26:9 and 11 the setting is of a woman anointing Jesus with expensive oil. The disciples condemn her before Jesus for wasting money. They admonish her, saying that she should have used the money to give to the poor (v. 9). Jesus defends her, saying, "You will always have the poor with you" (v. 11). This is another clear example of "poor" specifically referring to powerless people.[4]

In sum, "poor" refers to the materially poor, marginalized, and afflicted. Matthew shows full awareness of synonyms for *ptōchos*, which he uses to describe noneconomic and nonphysical affliction.

What does Jesus mean by adding "in spirit" to the poor? In the Greek translation of Psalm 33:19 (English 34:18) we have a similar phrase to "poor in spirit" with "crushed in spirit:" "The LORD is near to the brokenhearted, and saves the crushed [Greek: *tapeinous*, humble] in spirit." Important to my argument is that "in spirit" in this verse does not change the Greek *tapeinous* "crushed/humble/contrite." "In spirit" rather emphasizes the nature of being humble (*tapeinous*); in other words, it is like saying "extremely humble." This should make us more circumspect in assuming that "in spirit" alters the sense of "poor" (*ptōchos*) in the beatitude of Matthew 5:3. I propose that "in spirit" adds emphasis to the actual poverty of the poor rather than changing the meaning of the type of "poor" (*ptōchos*).

Jesus ends the first beatitude with "theirs is the kingdom of heaven." This is Matthew's distinctive way of speaking of God's reign on earth. Those who are starving and dying of thirst are now to be joyful because God's reign has begun in the actions of Jesus's healings, teachings, and transforming of the attitudes of those who are more materially wealthy (cf. Matthew 25:31–46).

Beatitude Two

Blessed are those who mourn, for they will be comforted.

Jesus here alludes to Isaiah 61:2–3:

> to comfort all who mourn; to provide for those who mourn in Zion—to give them a garland instead of ashes, the oil of gladness instead of mourning, the mantle of praise instead of a faint spirit.

Those who are mourning are the victims of the greed and violence especially of the arrogant and rich but also of those who have just enough but do not stand out against the policies of the rich and greedy. It is not only wretched humans who mourn, as Hosea observes:

> Swearing, lying, and murder, and stealing and adultery break out; bloodshed follows bloodshed. Therefore the land mourns, and all who live in it languish; together with the wild animals and the birds of the air, even the fish of the sea are perishing. (4:2–3)

God hears the cry of his whole creation. We have seen that in Scripture human sin does not just lead to human suffering but to environmental suffering. Unfaithfulness to God's commands to be generous inevitably leads to desertification, lack of fertile land, lack of water, and so on.

Beatitude Three

Blessed are the meek [Greek: praeis], for they will inherit the earth.

We must recognize Matthew 5:5 as referring back to the Greek translation of Psalm 36:11 (English 37:11):

> But the meek [Greek: *praeis*] shall inherit the land, and delight themselves in abundant prosperity. (37:11)

The meek in this psalm are those who have no power, wealth or land but hope for a time when their situation will be reversed. For this reason Artur Weiser translates the psalm: "But the humiliated shall inherit the land."[5] This is a position that Davies and Allison take, believing that *praeis* in Matthew 5:5 refers to the "powerless."[6] The powerless and humiliated are blessed right now in God's kingdom revealed in Jesus's re-creating work.

The staggering claim of the beatitude is that the "powerless" will inherit the earth. This earth is to be the scene of the coming kingdom of God. It could be argued that to Jesus's listeners, "earth" refers to the land of Israel, but "earth" usually equals all creation in the New Testament. Jesus's actions envisage God's reign beginning to transform the present in which the oppressed dwell. Jesus's word about inheriting the earth "challenges systems secured by Roman power which furthered the interests of local landowning elite at the expense of peasants forced into a subsistence existence."[7]

Beatitude Four

> Blessed are those who hunger and thirst for righteousness [Greek: *dikaiosunē*], for they will be filled.

Matthew refers seven times to *dikaiosunē* (3:15; 5:6, 10, 20; 6:1, 33; and 21:32). It is associated with doing justice and righting what is wrong. In other words, those who seek *dikaiosunē* desire "rightness" or righteousness. Some understandably argue that Jesus refers to "blessed are those who actively strive for justice for others."[8] I am not convinced and follow Carter, who sees Jesus as referring to those who are literally hungry and thirsty. Some people's actual bodily needs are denied because of a lack of "right societal relationships and access to adequate resources for living (5:5, land; 6:11, bread)."[9] It is not incidental that

Jesus uses "hunger" and "thirst" in this verse. Such language is misread by most people in economically developed countries who have never known real hunger and thirst.

In sum, God's "righteousness" which people hunger and thirst for is basic for their physical needs. If we visualize malnourished children with swollen bellies, we will be closer to whom Jesus is referring to. They cry out for God's help (Psalm 107:5–6).

Ecological Significance

My thinking about the relevance of the first four beatitudes for the ecological crisis is helped by Wangari Maathai's account of her return to her home in Kenya.

> I also learned that someone had acquired the piece of land where the fig tree I was in awe of as a child had stood. The new owner perceived the tree to be a nuisance because it took up much space and he felled it to make room for tea. By then I understood the connection between the tree and water, so it did not surprise me that when the fig tree was cut down, the stream where I had played with the tadpoles dried up. My children would never be able to play with frogs' eggs as I had or simply enjoy the cool, clean water of that stream. I mourned the loss of that tree. I profoundly appreciated the wisdom of my people, and how generations of women had passed on to their daughters the cultural tradition of leaving the fig trees in place.[10]

Maathai hears the voices of creation that cry out for justice. She sees the suffering that arises from a careless and ignorant chopping down of a fig tree. It is easy to be uninformed and take careless actions like this. Our cultures buttress us in our comfy places, protecting us from the cries of suffering. When we face uncomfortable truths, we find ways to hide from them.

Jesus refers to the cries and suffering of the powerless. We must hear them and use Maathai's words above as an example of someone in tune with Jesus's Beatitudes. My exegesis emphasizes how vital it is we understand our world so that we can hear the cries of the powerless as Maathai does. If we don't hear their cries, we cannot bring good news, and we will fail God and those who cry out. We must do all we can to see and hear the suffering of God's creation so that we can understand what it means for the poor to be blessed.

Finally, Maathai exemplifies one who sees connectedness in all creation. She perceives that the simple act of cutting down a fig tree leads to suffering and loss of joy to others. In embodying the Beatitudes, we too must deepen our sensitivity toward all creation and see the connectedness of all creation. We must pray to be aware of the consequences to our world of our every action, direct or indirect.

Chapter Summary

In the first four beatitudes, Jesus begins by emphasizing the afflicted and marginalized of our world. Jesus announces good news to them insofar as healing and reversal of their suffering are now at hand. But it follows that those "who have" must change so that they can bring joy and wholeness to the afflicted. It is mandatory for Christians to work toward the fair distribution of land and the cancellation of debts so that people can be free and work the land so that it abounds in life for themselves and their families.

Reflection Questions

1. To whom specifically do you think Jesus would be referring in these four beatitudes today?
2. How would you assess your awareness of their voices?
3. What kind of things cause affliction, other than natural catastrophes, to those who have nothing? Try to be specific.

Chapter 7

THE BEATITUDES 2: MATTHEW 5:7–12

In the previous chapter we saw that in the Beatitudes Jesus refers to people who suffer affliction. The first four beatitudes provide the necessary preliminaries for the beatitudes that follow. In beatitudes five to nine we read about those who seek justice for the powerless and voiceless.

It is necessary first to hear the cries of the poor in order to know how to respond. Those referred to in beatitudes five to nine are people who hear the voices of the afflicted. These beatitudes point to those who see and hear God and respond to him in bringing blessings and good news to the afflicted.

Our ministry in this time of ecological crisis should be enriched through a careful study of each of the beatitudes in Matthew 5:7–12. In doing so we must reflect on our own ministry in the light of those who are "blessed" so that we can become people of the Beatitudes.

Matthew 5:7–10

We find described in Matthew 5:7–10 people who stand in opposition to injustices done to God's creation. They are praised for living by values alternative to those of their world. We will now analyze each beatitude in more detail.

Beatitude Five

> Blessed are the merciful, for they will receive mercy.

In a merciless world Jesus teaches that justice can be established only by people practicing mercy and generosity. Those who forgive others will receive greater mercy from God. The psalmist claims that the one who seeks justice should expect wealth in his or her house because it is in giving to the poor that blessings come (Psalm 112:3, 9). Similarly, people of beatitude five will establish justice through mercy, because they will be rich in the gift of God's mercy.

Jesus teaches that those who show mercy are blessed in that they know themselves forgiven and released by God (see also Matthew 18:23–35). Such knowledge immediately shows itself in practical actions of mercy toward others. The importance of this is emphasized later in Matthew's gospel when Jesus reprimands the Pharisees in the strongest terms for not showing mercy (Matthew 23:23), thereby showing ignorance of God's Word and mercy.

Israel should have understood the importance of mercy and generosity. The Promised Land was to be a "compassionate kingdom" rooted in God's commandments. God told Israel that the well-being of its land and people depended on its obedience to him. Obedience meant embodying generosity and mercy. God gave the land to Israel so that it could exemplify to the nations how God intended people to live with each other and the land. The land provided the place for Israel's practical response to God's mercy and generosity, where it could build a compassionate society.

For the new Israel, the church, it is the whole earth, not just a small piece of land, where we are called to practice mercy. In the Jubilee regulations all Israelites were to share the same status before God, and they must show compassion for each other (Leviticus 25:35, 40, 53). Today this is extended to all creation, and Christians who believe they are the objects of God's compassion must extend compassion to others.

Ecological Significance. Showing compassion must be embodied in political and economic terms. Today economic debt affects many poor nations. Poor countries pay over $157 million every day to the rich world in debt repayments, rather than spending the money on vital health care and education.[1] Maathai commenting on her country of Kenya argues that "poverty was not only the result of bad government and environmental mismanagement, but also an outcome of the global economic systems, one of the key realities of which, for poor countries, was crippling debts."[2] She observes that between 1970 and 2002, African countries obtained about $540 billion (US) in loans and paid back $550 billion. Maathai points out that "because of interest on debt, by the end of 2002, the debtor countries still owed the lending agencies nearly $300 billion."[3]

The UN estimates that 7 million children die unnecessarily each year, from diseases that can be cured and from unclean water that could be made safe. If money that poor countries pay to the rich world in debt service was spent instead on tackling poverty and associated issues such as water supply, the lives of millions of children in poor countries would be saved.[4]

The lack of mercy and compassion that leads to debt also leads to ecological destruction. Bishop Peter Selby observes direct connection between indebtedness and the rate of deforestation. He notes, for example, that Brazil in the 1980s, leading the ranks of international debtors, increased its rate of deforestation by 245 percent.[5] Showing mercy toward other living creatures is thus inextricably linked to showing mercy to land, water, and air.

Beatitude Six

Blessed are the pure in heart, for they will see God.

Jesus teaches that those whose hearts are pure are blessed, for they will see God. The pure in heart perceive the world through God's eyes because their wills are in harmony with God. They will see God in their own actions of showing mercy to the afflicted. The pure in heart are thus revealed as those who show compassion. The pure in heart live with the presence of God constantly before them.

What is an "impure heart"? Three texts come to mind: Matthew 23:24; 15:1–20; and 25:31–46. In Matthew 23:24, Jesus rebukes the Jerusalem scribes and Pharisees for claiming that they are pure. Instead, Jesus condemns them for being full of plunder and self-indulgence (Matthew 23:25). Plunder and self-indulgence define our lifestyles in the West, as well as the worldview that empowered Rome and its economic policies. "Plunder" refers to violation of neighbors by robbery (Leviticus 6:2); to imperial oppression by violent attack, exile, and slaughter; and to the acts of the leaders and policymakers who take away the rights of the poor, orphans, and widows and take their goods for themselves. Jesus condemns the misuse of power to dominate and oppress others for one's own benefit (Matthew 21:13). "Self-indulgence" suggests lack of control referring to the inability to delay gratification. In contrast, Jesus in the wilderness fasts and lives a life of simplicity and self-control. The heart of Jesus was pure and was not set on money and wealth (Matthew 6:25–31) but on bringing good news to those who have nothing.

In Matthew 15:1–20, Jesus teaches that what is unclean is what proceeds from the heart and is acted out: "For out of the heart come evil intentions, murder, adultery, fornication, theft, false witness, slander. These are what defile a person" (Matthew 15:19–20). Jesus thus refers to social actions, as well as evil intentions, as impure.

In Matthew 25:31–46, the parable of the sheep and the goats, the sheep that care for the afflicted are said to be those who are blessed. Although pure and impure are not mentioned, it is evident that the sheep are contrasted with the goats to show what it is to be pure. The word "blessed" here is different from the word used in the Beatitudes. Those who care for the afflicted are not blessed in the sense of "joyful" but blessed in the sense of touched by God. It is important to note that those who are blessed are surprised at being blessed, for although they saw God, they did not recognize God in the unlikely form of the hungry, thirsty, alien, naked, sick, and prisoner.

Christopher Rowland has suggested that at the heart of the parable of the sheep and the goats is a polemic against those who thought they were "blessed" because of their preoccupation with "heaven."[6] These are represented as the goats that are "cursed" because they did not care for the afflicted and marginalized (see Deuteronomy 28:15–68). Matthew's wording suggests that they were too caught up in other things to see God in the afflicted. Indeed, this is alluded to in Jesus's response to John the Baptist's disciples as they sought to find out if Jesus was the Messiah. His messiahship, he tells them, is evident in his concern for the afflicted (Matthew 11:5) and not in heavenly speculation. The Pharisees failed to recognize the coming of God's reign in Jesus's concern for the poor. As we have seen, Jesus denounces them for their neglect of the poor (Matthew 23:23).

Ecological Significance. Plunder and self-indulgence bring destruction to God's creation. For the first time in history we are realizing that the earth cannot sustain our plunder or inability to use restraint. Oil is becoming an issue of concern for governments of economically leading nations. There is evidence and acknowledgment that we have or soon will have used up more than half the planet's oil supplies and that from now on oil is going to be harder to get and more expensive. For example, Thierry Desmarest, chairman of Total, the world's fourth largest oil company, declared that production would peak by around 2020. He urged governments to find ways to suppress oil demand growth and put off the witching hour.[7] Just about everything we consume involves oil, for example: aspirin, adhesive tape, trainer shoes, Lycra socks, CDs, DVDs, plastic bottles, contact lenses, and so on. The list is endless. Former UK prime minister Tony Blair says, "Fuel is our economic lifeblood. The price of oil can be the difference between recession and recovery. The Western world is import-dependent."[8] We appear not to have the resources to survive without oil.

This crisis is one that calls Christians to give witness to being pure in heart. Jesus says that to be "pure in heart" is to seek a way of life based on care and generosity involving restraint. We must assess how we can cut back on our use of oil and encourage others to do so.

To avoid the catastrophes that could result from lack of oil, such as power shortages, lack of fuel for transport, inability to maintain technology and manufacturing and even war, limits will need to be observed.

We still have a chance to change and to live according to God's laws. If we do not choose to limit ourselves, some day we will be forced to change anyway, just in order to survive. The issue of declining oil tells us that we consume too much and that we are too dependent on something that we cannot guarantee will be around for future generations. I believe that to be pure in heart is to see the situation as God sees it and the dangers ahead. This means that we need to learn to rely less on oil.

Being "pure in heart" is also related to showing mercy, as in the previous beatitude. Our desire in the West for oil has caused great pollution and suffering to many oil-producing nations. The people who live in the Niger Delta, for example, have had to live with environmental catastrophes for decades caused by producing oil for developed nations. In a recent article for the UK's leading newspaper, the *Observer*, environment editor John Vidal writes of his trip to Nigeria: "Forest and farmland were now covered in a sheen of greasy oil. Drinking wells were polluted and people were distraught. No one knew how much oil had leaked. 'We lost our nets, huts and fishing pots' said Chief Promise, village leader of Otuegwe and our guide. 'This is where we fished and farmed. We have lost our forest. We told Shell of the spill within days, but they did nothing for six months.'"[9]

Vidal's article illustrates the extent to which greed leads to oppression and suffering for others, as well as to environmental devastation. Yet showing mercy and being pure in heart require ensuring the poor and afflicted do not suffer unduly. In the context of the issue of declining oil, then, we must adapt our lifestyles not for our own sakes, but because this is best for the poor and the environment. Using less oil will mean improvements for nations like Nigeria where pollution and poor working conditions have devastated the poorest of those nations, wrecking their ability to work and feed themselves.

Beatitude Seven

Blessed are the peacemakers, for they will be called children of God.

The word "peacemaker" seems such an imprecise term that we can be tempted to miss the importance of "peace" words in the New Testament. We must look at what peace is in Jesus's teachings.

The Hebrew word for "peace" is *shalom* and describes a state of harmony throughout all creation that God works toward. Peace is not keeping your head down and avoiding stirring things up. Peace is not forever smiling and being nice and polite to people. Jesus has not come to bring a message about being "nice" upon earth, but what he teaches will result in strife represented in the word "sword" (Matthew 10:34). It is surely not coincidental that another similar occurrence of the noun "peacemaker" is found in Proverbs 10:10: "The one who rebukes boldly makes peace." In other words, peacemaking is not to maintain the status quo. For Proverbs 10:10 peacemakers are more akin to "disturbers of the status quo."

Jesus was not a man who kept his head down, avoiding trouble. He is a good example of a peacemaker in the tradition taught in Proverbs 10:10. He had no concern, for example, at upsetting the people in the synagogue in Nazareth (Luke 4). He shows impatience and irritation toward his disciples (Matthew 17:17). Elsewhere Jesus calls the leaders "vipers," "fools," "hypocrites," and "blind guides" (Matthew 23).

Why then is Jesus described as a quiet man who did not break a bruised reed or cry aloud in the marketplace (Matthew 12:19–21)? It is true that he did not engage in certain and irrelevant disputes to defend his identity and credentials.[10] Yet Matthew points specifically to Jesus's care for the poor who suffer through hard manual labor and lack of nutrition and resources by noting that he does not "break a bruised reed" or "quench a smouldering wick." Toward them Jesus is compassionate with healings, exorcisms, and the formation of an alternative community.[11] To the poor, Jesus is indeed a gentle and compassionate man. Central to being a peacemaker is therefore giving and sharing with those who are marginalized and deprived and rebuking boldly those who have too much.

Jesus further teaches that the peacemakers will be called "children of God," therefore being at one with the will of God and seeking that will that is to bring peace; "children of God" are like their Father in heaven by loving their enemies (Matthew 5:44–45). The merciful and pure in heart are the peacemakers who live the life of Jubilee in the knowledge that what they have is given by God and that it is for all. They see God, know God intimately as their very life source, and therefore share generously with others.

Peace in the Old and New Testaments is the content of the good news (Isaiah 52:7a) and the salvation in which God's reign is revealed.[12] To be a peacemaker is not a garment to put on and off when it suits. It is the necessary and unconditional task of being a follower of God.

Ecological Significance. We live in a society where self-interest is elevated above interest for others. Being "peacemakers" sums up what it means to be Christians in this world. This must translate into action. At a social level this means working toward sharing creation with those who are deprived of land, food, water, and shelter. This is central to God's covenant given to aid humanity to work for a peaceable kingdom where God's creation is teeming with life.

In sharing, our own security is threatened. When God commands that on the seventh year Israelites must let the land rest, he is challenging them to demonstrate their trust that he will care for them. If peacemaking is connected with Jubilee, giving to the vulnerable is central.

I suggest that to pursue this kind of life is to draw forth the wrath of society. Peacemakers are those who do not stand back but who act courageously (Proverbs 10:10). Christians must, therefore, configure new ways of life that care for the poor and marginalized, and this cannot be done unless they consider the suffering cry of the whole of creation.

We saw in our discussion of beatitude six, that the rich nations' dependency on oil causes conflict in our world. This is also the case with water. It is thought that by 2050 nearly half of the world's population will face severe water shortages.[13] With such shortages is it not surprising that competition for water is increasing.[14] I quote Valerio at length:

The economic demands placed on poorer countries by the rich nations include privatisation of public amenities. As a result, water prices are hiked up in the cities, and the needs of those in urban areas are ignored. Water problems are growing, too, because of the increasing consumption of water due to economic development and higher standards of living. The tourism industry, for example, can worsen shortages as hotels and golf courses take the majority of water away from the local community. Industry and agriculture consume huge amounts of water (agriculture uses 70% of the world's water). They lead to deforestation, soil erosion, and water pollution, all of which exacerbate water problems.[15]

We cannot survive without water. As peacemakers we must address this issue because it affects the poor and the environment. If we are to prevent wars occurring over water, we must look at our own use of water that puts demands on others. Recently I was talking to a church minister who supports action on ecological issues, and in passing he told me he had been golfing in a foreign country. The foreign country was short of water. It is so easy for us to ignore the consequences of our actions. The creation of a golf course not only creates water problems, but also takes away valuable land that could be used for growing food. Further, golf courses can mean loss of biodiversity.

Beatitude Eight

> Blessed are those who are persecuted for righteousness' sake, for theirs is the kingdom of heaven.

In the previous chapter I considered the fourth beatitude about those who hunger and thirst for righteousness. I proposed that it referred to those who actually lack basic sustenance. Beatitude eight, however, points to those who, because of showing mercy, being pure in heart, and being peacemakers, will be persecuted. Jesus compares those who are persecuted to the Old Testament prophets who also were persecuted because of their desire

- To establish God's intention for the poor (5:3)

- To comfort those who weep (5:4)
- To give land to the humiliated (5:5)

Jesus teaches in the eighth beatitude that his disciples must accept persecution and not give up, accommodate, or retaliate. Those who seek justice must be ready to encounter many setbacks, but in facing these they will rejoice in knowing that their unpopularity comes through acting according to God's will.

The phrase "kingdom of heaven," which appears in verses 3 and 10, reveals the unity between the first four beatitudes and beatitudes five to eight. Beatitudes five to eight complete the symmetry of the eight beatitudes with the last four beatitudes corresponding implicitly to the first four. This parallel structure shows that those who seek cosmic justice work for fair distribution of God's creation to all and that God's reign is present in such work and is evident in the removal of poverty.

Ecological Significance. This beatitude calls "joyous" those whose actions make them unpopular. In the Philippines in November 2008, journalist Aristeo Padriago had his face blown off in front of his seven-year-old daughter after he had been vocal in his attack on local politicians' involvement in illegal logging.[16] Similarly, Khim Sambo and his son were gunned down in the street in Cambodia because of their work against illegal logging. Arbi Kusno was attacked by a mob believed to be working for timber smugglers armed with spears, machetes, and hydrochloric acid. In Mexico in 2007, twenty-year-old activist Aldo Zamora was gunned down by assassins angry at his opposition to logging in the Tlahuica indigenous community. These are a few examples of people standing out and resisting those involved in harming creation. In contrast, Christians in affluent situations are often apathetic and wouldn't dream of risking life and limb for the goal of establishing cosmic justice.

We should remember these courageous examples of considering the Beatitudes and working toward cosmic justice and adjust our own consumption patterns accordingly. Those involved in fighting illegal logging die because there is a demand for such logging. The UK, for example, spends a staggering £712 ($1109) million annually on illegal wood products. That is £11.96 ($18.63) per person.[17] As Andrew Wasley reminded us previously, when we "queue up to buy tables, chairs, cabinets, blinds, and other similar, seemingly innocent and unremarkable items," we must remember the suffering behind their production.

Summary Beatitude: Verses 11–12

> Blessed are you when people revile you and persecute you and utter all kinds of evil against you falsely on my account. Rejoice and be glad, for your reward is great in heaven, for in the same way they persecuted the prophets who were before you.

This beatitude summarizes the previous beatitudes and brings them home personally to Jesus's major audience then and now: his disciples.[18] In these verses there is a change from the pronoun "they" to "you." Jesus is now referring to his close disciples. This specifically addresses Christians.

In the previous eight beatitudes, Jesus speaks more distantly about the poor and those who remove poverty. Jesus sets out the horror of a society that allows poverty and then moves to describe the necessary characteristics of those who would reverse the fortunes of the poor. Now, suddenly and abruptly, Jesus makes eye contact with those few disciples standing before him and says, "Blessed are you when . . . ." This is a dramatic scene. One could well imagine being one of those disciples and looking at the ground when Jesus addressed you with the phrase "Blessed are you when . . . ." The disciples are challenged and told that they will be joyous only when they are reviled and persecuted and when people slander them on account of Jesus. "When" suggests being "blessed" is conditional on being reviled.

In the ninth beatitude the disciples are no longer doers as in beatitudes five to seven but are like the victims in beatitudes one to four.[19] However, there is a big difference; they are not victims in the sense of the first four beatitudes as they have chosen their way of life. It is their choice to bring justice and to be always active in transforming the situation of poverty. Cosmic justice mentioned in the ninth beatitude is synonymous with Jesus, who is always acting to bring justice. In verse 12 Jesus compares his disciples to the prophets, who also were not victims or passive. They acted boldly on behalf of the oppressed and marginalized. In so acting they empowered the voiceless and acted together to redistribute God's creation on the basis of need rather than some abstract human understanding of "merit."

Ecological Significance. When Jesus says, "Blessed are you when . . ." it must have a direct impact on us. It is no longer the less personal "Blessed are those . . . for they will be . . . ." Now Jesus is talking directly to us.

It is easy to be assimilated into the consumer societies in which we live. How do we avoid this? This is a question I have heard many ask in Western societies. First, we must establish goals in a realistic and achievable way. Some may be able to live without a car, for example; others can't but might be able to cut down on miles traveled. Some might decide that they can become vegetarian, but others might decide to cut down on their meat consumption. It might be that those who love shopping might attempt to shop more ecologically and ethically. They could perhaps support charity shops or shops that sell fair-trade products from less-developed nations.

Second, it is important that we form small networks to support each other, sharing our attempts at living more ecologically. For example, after a summer school on ecology and the Bible, my students formed an e-mail network, supporting each other in living more compassionately with the poor and the earth. People are doing small things like cutting back on the number of canned foods they use, cutting down on meat and/or coffee; others are thinking of buying more eco-friendly cars, while some are trying to grow their own vegetables.

As well as assessing our consuming tendencies and supporting each other, we must also consider how far we should go in responding to the injustices we see carried out. In our society many of us find it inconceivable to think of dying as an ultimate form of resistance to injustice. However, each of us needs to listen to the personal address of Jesus to act for cosmic justice without concern as to what the consequence will be. It is important that we seek to challenge people in positions of power on issues relating to using illegal wood, selling of non-fair-trade chocolate, improving public transport, encouraging more bike-friendly paths, planting trees, and so on. We can encourage our churches to cut back on their energy bills and to use any land they have more ecologically. These activities may not get us sent to prison, but they are still countercultural and determined actions that we must persistently and patiently engage in.

Chapter Summary

Mercy begins this chapter and rightly so. "Showing mercy" sums up God and what Christians should aspire to. Ecologically we must seek to relate to all creation in a way that alleviates suffering and brings hope. We must encourage our leaders to develop economic and consumption polices that are more giving to those oppressed and afflicted and more realistic about what planet Earth can sustain.

As those who are pure in heart, we should strive to see and desire nothing other than what God desires. To be pure in heart is to see oneself as dependent on God and on the rest of his creation. It is also to see ourselves as sinners, repent, and live more merciful lives.

As peacemakers, we must engage in activities that reveal the causes of conflict and suffering and suggest actions at local and global levels that can bring peace.

Lastly, while we do not desire to be persecuted, to be Christian in a world where there is injustice cannot be easy. We must be proactive to bring about a world that sustains all living creatures.

Reflection Questions

1. There are 1 billion people who cannot meet their basic consumption requirements. Can we be "blessed" when such inequality exists?
2. In reflecting on beatitudes five to nine, how can we be aware of the institutions, policies, and processes that create inequalities and poverty? What can we do to transform them?

3. Who are the individuals and groups that are persecuted for seeking cosmic justice?

Chapter 8

THE LORD'S PRAYER 1: MATTHEW 6:9–10

Most Christians are familiar with the Lord's Prayer. Indeed, it is likely that many have committed it to memory. In my treatment of this prayer I hope that familiarity will not breed complacency but will be the basis of a daily refreshing of our whole being for radical action to the benefit of all creation. Dividing our examination of the Lord's Prayer into two chapters will help us consider the petitions on their own terms.

Carter comments that the Lord's Prayer looks to God to respond both now and in the future and through the lives and practices of disciples. Praying is part of, not removed from or a substitute for, the lived faithfulness of disciples.[1] To pray the Lord's Prayer is to act in a way that puts the one who prays into an alternative way of living, becoming a disturber of the status quo.

The Lord's Prayer is a real jewel both in teaching Christians how to pray and in instructing them about Jesus's understanding of his mission on earth as he perceived it. In this chapter and the following I argue that to pray the Lord's Prayer calls us to pray in a way that means taking action and showing our commitment to the words of prayer we utter. I believe that this means rethinking our lifestyles and our relationships both to each other and to the rest of creation.

Literary Structure

Matthew 6:9–13 is divided into two parts. The first part has three petitions with the word "your" (vv. 9–10):

- Hallowed be your name.
- Your kingdom come.
- Your will be done, on earth as it is in heaven.

Part two has three further petitions with the word "our" or "us" (vv. 11–13):

- Give us this day our daily bread.
- And forgive us our debts, as we also have forgiven our debtors.
- And do not bring us to the time of trial, but rescue us from the evil one.

The prayer stands at the center of Jesus's Sermon on the Mount. The most immediate context is Jesus teaching his disciples not to pray by heaping up empty phrases. He emphasizes that God knows what is needed before it is requested (Matthew 6:8). This suggests a polemic side to Jesus's teaching in which prayer is not said for approval or to be successful. Carter comments that "employing polemical language, this section contrasts the disciples' lifestyle with the piety of both the synagogue (Jews) and the Greco-Roman world."[2] For example, Carter observes that "the petition for daily bread, for instance, is, for those with plenty, a petition against greed and luxury."[3]

Our Father

Matthew repeatedly brings up the idea of the fatherhood of God.[4] The personal pronoun "our" in the phrase "our Father" emphasizes the sense of intimacy the praying person has with God. We will consider ideas associated with the word "father" in the Old and the New Testaments.

"Our Father" speaks of the originator of all things (Isaiah 64:8; cf. Job 10:9),[5] as well as defining the relationship of God to the rest of creation. The book of Job, for example, emphasizes that God is Father to all creation (Job 38:28). In Psalm 103:13–14 God is a compassionate Father who knows how all things were made. This very Father is the one who remembers that all are dust. "Father" suggests that God continues to be present for his whole creation in contrast to the clock maker who stops caring about the clock once it is ticking.

"Father" is not a common way of referring to God in the Old Testament, but on occasions where it does occur, it tells us a lot about God.

In the Psalms, God is the Father of orphans and protector of widows (Psalm 68:5). The king himself will also cry, "You are my Father, my God, and the Rock of my salvation!" (Psalm 89:26). In Psalm 103:13, God is compared to a compassionate father for his children. In Isaiah 9:6, we read, "For a child has been born for us, a son given to us; authority rests upon his shoulders; and he is named Wonderful Counselor, Mighty God, Everlasting Father, Prince of Peace." This is a description of the hoped-for king who will bring justice to Israel. He is God's representative in all things. Associated with being "Everlasting Father" are ideas of counselor, peace, and power. In Isaiah 63:16, God is known as Father and Redeemer, again reinforcing him as an affectionate and compassionate Father.

When we turn to the New Testament, we find much that tells us about God as Father. Kenneth E. Bailey, in his book, *Jesus through Middle Eastern Eyes*, shows how Luke's account of Jesus's parable about the prodigal son (Luke 15:11–32) defines what Jesus means by "our Father" and in a way that relates to the Old Testament ideas above. Bailey writes, "In that story Jesus breaks all bounds of human patriarchy and presents an image of a father that goes beyond anything his culture expected from any human father."[6] According to Bailey's study, the prodigal's father is the portrait of God, whose goodness, love, forgiveness, care, and compassion have no limits at all. God is a giver of property, compassion, and generosity. In the parable God (the father) seeks to bring about the son's repentance by showing compassion and forgiveness. He allows him, albeit with great sadness, to make mistakes so that he can see for himself the suffering that follows such acts.

In Matthew, God is compared to a father who gives to his children: "If you then, who are evil, know how to give good gifts to your children, how much more will your Father in heaven give good things to those who ask him!" (Matthew 7:11). This ordinary example of a father giving to his children argues for an understanding of how much more God will give. Similarly in Matthew 18:12–14, God is like a shepherd who leaves the ninety-nine sheep to seek the one sheep that is lost.

God is a Father who acts compassionately to lead his children to see how much they need him, as well as how all things belong to him. There are no special or favored people before God; we are all connected by being "created." Therefore, in praying, "Our Father," we should be humbled before him however beautiful, clever, skilled, and productive we are. We created beings belong to each other and to everything around us, including the soil, air, rivers, and seas.

In praying, "Our Father," we confess the oneness of all creation before God acknowledging our sense of belonging to everything around us. This is unlike the prodigal son, who believed himself independent and accountable to no one. In praying, "Our Father," we stop thinking of ourselves as being "owners" who have belongings, for this Father is the father of the whole of creation, and everything belongs to him. Like us, the birds and springs, oaks and beeches praise God in their distinctive ways. We are all partners and together praising God while awaiting final transformation (Genesis 9:9–10; Romans 8:19–23).[7]

In praying, "Our Father," we are also like the prodigal son, realizing that we have abused our Father in ignoring and rejecting our obligations and duties to him, especially in neglecting the needs of the poor. Like the son we recognize that we are dependent on God for all we have. God forgives his children and seeks to transform them by love and compassion so that they can extend such compassion to each other. In declaring, "Our Father," we acknowledge that we are owned and that we must seek to live in the honor of belonging to God by seeking to be like him, working for cosmic justice.

Ecological Significance. In confessing God as "our Father," we acknowledge ourselves as created. We are to see those around us not as commodities to be used for our own purposes but as our fellow created brothers and sisters with the same Father. Sadly, the words "Our Father" are so familiar that we often miss this meaning. We are also so disconnected from a first-century agrarian context that we think it has relevance only to humans. If we were not so disconnected, we would understand our relationship with the whole of creation and look more compassionately on it.

Therefore, we must treat the whole of creation as brothers and sisters. Francis of Assisi, the thirteenth-century saint, understood better than most the idea that to declare God as "our Father" is to realize that all creation is both our brother and our sister. In Francis's "The Canticle of Brother Sun" he writes:

> All praise be yours, my Lord, through all that you have made,
> And first my lord Brother Sun,
> Who brings the day; and light you give us through him.[8]

Francis shows a kinship with all creation. Throughout the lines of the canticle he acknowledges his gratitude toward not only "Brother Sun," but also "Sister Moon and stars" (line 10), "Wind and Air" (line 15), and "Fire" (line 17). Francis lived as Jesus did in the wilderness, living lightly on earth. Franciscan brother Ramon observes that, like Jesus, Francis had no place to lay his head, and Francis took from the earth only what was necessary for sustaining life, in contrast to our consumer society.[9] Ramon further observes, "In Francis, there is a divine call to love, embracing both nature and neighbour in a healing and reconciling union that is the pattern both for ecology and political relationships throughout the world."[10]

To say, "Our Father," means we need to get to know our brothers and sisters. Perhaps some of us are so out of touch with nature that our sense of kinship with it has almost disappeared. To address this I have committed myself increasingly to growing my own vegetables in order to get to know the land. I was also inspired by many of my students in Tanzania who combined their studies with working the land. Similarly, Echlin observes, "Every neighbourhood and every town, like every garden, is distinct and unique. Getting to know one's local soils, flora, and fauna, seasonal migrants, and local food and drink in its distinctiveness, is one of the pleasures of a lifetime."[11]

"Our Father" is not only my Father but the Father of all. Saying and understanding the words "Our Father" commit us to act in an ecologically responsible way. We each must ask what we must do so that we can be better connected not only with other humans but also with the rest of creation. Echlin offers good advice:

> Earth *abuse* is a grave structural evil requiring repentance by all of us. Restitution for the injustice of earth abuse, injustice to the whole earth community, means, for example, that we literally must remove some pavement and roll back asphalt with which for decades we have crushed the earth. Each of us in our neighbourhoods can heal the sorry "state we are in" by removing some slabs, concrete or pavement from near our homes, churches, offices, and schools, letting life live again. For many of us this means we can perhaps remove an inch, others can lift whole slabs, still others can help to reforest military airfield and automobile graveyard.[12]

Who Is in the Heavens

Twenty times Matthew modifies "Father" with some form of the word "heaven." This is particularly distinctive when "Father in heaven" occurs elsewhere only in Mark 11:25.

Matthew can refer to "heaven" both in the singular and in the plural. In 6:9 it is in the plural, meaning it refers to the divine/invisible realm.[13] Jesus implies God's realm is in heaven.[14] He is not only loving Father, but also almighty God. Bruner comments, "Lest we become too chummy with "our Father," the qualifier "in the heavens" tells us that this Father is *God*. And lest we become too selfish with the Father, "in heavens" tells us that God is not only in my sky but in all the skies of the world."[15]

Ecological Significance. The fact that God is in heaven reminds us that we are not God. We are created beings on earth to whom God relates from above. We must keep before us daily that "God is in heaven and humans are not." We should not think ourselves more special to God than the rest of creation.

Hallowed Be Your Name

The Old Testament states that humanity profanes God through its inability to be what God created it to be. In Ezekiel 36:16–23, Israel is told that it had defiled the land by shedding blood and worshiping idols. In Leviticus 22:31–32, Israel is commanded to sanctify God's name through its obedience to him and his commandments. In Isaiah 29:23, God's name will be sanctified when his works are seen. The crucial point is that when God's works are seen his name is hallowed.

The Old Testament says that the rest of creation sanctifies God's name by praising him. The psalmist states that "all your works shall give thanks to you, O LORD" (Psalm 145:10, cf. v. 5; 148:13; 150:6). Bauckham comments that "all creatures bring glory to God simply by being themselves and fulfilling their God-given roles in creation."[16] By implication nonhuman creation praises God and therefore honors his name, whereas humanity dishonors his name in not being as God intended.

We read that humanity brings dishonor to God's name by preventing the rest of creation from exalting his name. This is seen when the rest of creation cries out to God for its suffering caused by human sin (Hosea 4.3). Another good example is Isaiah 24:4–5: "The earth dries up and withers, the world languishes and withers; the heavens languish together with the earth. The earth lies polluted under its inhabitants; for they have transgressed laws, violated the statutes, broken the everlasting covenant."

In sum, Jesus instructs his disciples about prayer, knowing that all creation is God's work and that it sanctifies God's name in being itself.

However, to pray these words is to live in such a way that praises God's name and allows all creation to praise him.

Ecological Significance. We could paraphrase the petition: "Please make your real identity known so that we and others will recognize and honor you as you really are."[17] When we pray, "Let your name be sanctified," we are confessing that God's name is being profaned in our unecological actions. We must actively respond to God's hope for his future completed creation by doing our part to help creation hallow God's name. To honor God is to love him but also to love the creation he has made; these are the two great commandments upon which all the other commandments are based.

Your Kingdom Come

The hope of God's future kingdom of cosmic justice is what should drive human action even when such action seems futile. Like Jesus, we look forward to "the renewal of all things" (Matthew 19:28),[18] a new age and world, a new heaven and earth.

We pray for such a renewal, a renewal connected to the reversal of poverty. Isaiah 52:7 helps us understand what Jesus means by "kingdom of God." In an Aramaic translation with which Jesus would have been familiar, the phrase "Your God reigns" in the Hebrew of Isaiah 52:7 is paraphrased as "the kingdom of God is revealed."[19] In other words, when cosmic justice is brought about, the kingdom of God is revealed. Salvation is intricately connected with release and healing from social, ecological, and personal sin and debt.

Ecological Significance. Wendell Berry writes of three principles underlying the kingdom of God:

> The first principle of the Kingdom of God is that it includes everything; in it, the fall of every sparrow is a significant event. We are in it whether we know it or not and whether we wish to be or not. Another principle, both ecological and traditional, is that everything in the Kingdom of God

is joined both to it and to everything else that is in it; that is to say, the Kingdom of God is orderly. A third principle is that humans do not and can never know either all the creatures that the Kingdom of God contains or the whole pattern or order by which it contains them.[20]

In reflecting on the three principles Berry highlights, we are forced to think ecologically about what it means to pray, "Your kingdom come." When we pray, "Your kingdom come," we reorient our hope for the future in the light of God's promises for the completion of creation. This hope is not to be based on capital gain but the realization of cosmic justice on earth in which all God's creation can sanctify the name of its Creator. This must be done through humans living by the restraints placed on them by God so that harmony can exist between humans and the rest of creation.

Your Will Be Done on Heaven and Earth

Just as God the Father dwells in heaven, Jesus dwells on earth, revealing the nature of God and his will as it is done in heaven. Jesus addresses God as "Father, Lord of heaven and earth" (Matthew 11:25). He says that "all things" have been given to him by his Father. Jesus says that no one can know the Father except through him. When we remember that Jesus is a created being who dwells not in heaven but in Galilee, we see that God is thus revealed in created matter. God dwells on earth in Jesus.

The Greek for "all things" suggests far more than humanity. Jürgen Moltmann warns that "we cannot think of the one as over against or superior to the other. We can only talk about the fellowship and community of God's created beings."[21] There is equality in all creation since all, human and nonhuman, are God's creation.

Ecological Significance. "Your will be done" tells us that God's will is far from being done on earth. Presently on earth there is elitism, imperialism, militarism, and materialism, and these are not God's will. Yet earth has possibilities, and we hope and pray that in the future earth will experience the joys of heaven, the sphere of God's creative potentialities and energies.[22]

Disciples who pray, "Your will be done," recognize the pain and weeping of earth. The petition must be read alongside the hope that all creation, heaven and earth, will be the theater of God's glory. Moltmann expresses it well: "For created beings, this means that—all together, each created being in its own way—they will participate in eternal life and in the eternal bliss of the God who is present among them."[23]

If Christians have any doubts that God's desires for earth are good, then this petition should banish such doubts. Yet Moltmann observes how Christians still tend to think of "on earth as it is in heaven" as a longing to go to heaven; he notes that lack of care for the earth comes from our hope to leave earth behind.[24] Bailey comments that such escapist theology is far from what Jesus is calling us to pray for:

> Ecology, peace among peoples and nations, economic justice, racial equality, and refugees and land rights are all political issues that have to do with *this world* and are thus beyond the scope of the concerns of the Christian faith. But such is not the case if we pray "thy kingdom come, thy will be done *on earth*."[25]

Chapter Summary

We have examined the first three petitions. God as "Our Father" suggests that God is Creator of all creation. However, the fact that the Father is "in heaven" should lead us away from thinking of God as our buddy or ourselves as gods. When we praise God's name, we must recall that it is his intention for us to do so through obedience to his will. This means we must not through sin prevent the rest of creation from praising God. The mention of God's kingdom brings to mind God's promise to Israel of a Promised Land where cosmic justice reigns. To pray this prayer is to act in ways motivated by the hope of God's future completed creation with its abundance of life.

Reflection Questions

1. To what extent is your understanding of "Our Father" limited by a personal and human father? How does the Bible challenge this view?
2. Discuss ways of making the saying of the Lord's Prayer less familiar and more challenging.
3. Discuss what kinds of actions Christians can participate in that honor the first three petitions of the Lord's Prayer.

Chapter 9

THE LORD'S PRAYER 2: MATTHEW 6:11–13

In the previous chapter we saw how the first three petitions of the Lord's Prayer emphasize God as the key to understanding how we are to live within human community and with the rest of the world. God is Father of all; his dwelling is beyond our own, and his name is praised throughout his creation.

Christians who vocalize these words must also embody them in their everyday lives. We do this by praising God's name and bringing about his will on earth; also, through trusting and thanking God for his daily provisions and for his protection in the trials we face resulting from living this prayer.

In this chapter we consider Matthew 6:11–13, where we have three more petitions.

- Give us this day our daily bread.
- And forgive us our debts, as we also have forgiven our debtors.
- And do not bring us to the time of trial, but rescue us from the evil one.

The focus of the prayer is now on the praying person trusting God and living in ways that confess God as Creator. When we pray for our needs, we do so to praise God as our provider, not assuming we have any right to what we ask for.

Give Us Bread

Jesus teaches his disciples to acknowledge their need for food, so showing their trust in God to provide for them through his fruitful creation. The need to trust God is further emphasized in the same chapter as the Lord's Prayer when Jesus says, "Do not worry about your life, what you will eat or what you will drink" (Matthew 6:25), or when he says, "You cannot serve God and wealth" (Matthew 6:24). Bailey comments: *"All bread comes as a gift.*[1] It is not a right and we have not created it. Such gifts are in trust for the one who gives them. All material possessions are on loan from the owner; the God who created matter itself. This perspective on the material world is critical for the joyful life commended in the Gospels."[2]

Carter suggests that we read "Give us bread" alongside Proverbs 30:8: "Give me neither poverty nor riches; feed me with the food that I need."[3] Therefore, in praying for "bread," Jesus's disciples are not praying for any more than is necessary. Jesus teaches his disciples to live lightly on earth, trusting God for their sustenance. If our lives are dominated by storing up more than we need, we live as though independent of God (cf. 1 Timothy 6:8); Jesus emphatically teaches this in his parable of the rich fool who stores up more than is necessary (Luke 12:13–21).

In praying, "Give us bread," together, the disciples are forming a different community—in which bread is shared, the homeless housed, the naked clothed, and the divided reconciled (cf. Isaiah 58:6–7).[4] A community that prays to God for its food would hardly deny other brothers and sisters food when they needed it (cf. James 2:15). To live lightly on earth is to trust in others for their hospitality and to offer hospitality.

Ecological Significance. It is well documented that many of us devour our food mindlessly unaware of what we are eating. Further, we cook our synthetic packaged food in a microwave, eat some of it, and throw what remains in the trash. How can we pray with any sense of awareness to God for our food when we just take our food for granted? Like many of you, I have eaten more than I need, thrown away more than I should, failed to remember what I have eaten while failing to taste it, and never given a thought to the processes involved in getting this food to me on this plate.

If we are to pray with any level of integrity, "Give us today our daily bread," then we must adjust our lives to embody the sentiments of the words. I find Wendell Berry's comments helpful:

> Eating with the fullest pleasure—pleasure, that is, that does not depend on ignorance—is perhaps the profoundest enactment of our connection with the world. In pleasure we experience and celebrate our dependence and our gratitude, for we are living from mystery, from creatures we did not make and power we cannot comprehend.[5]

In thinking practically how we might develop more pleasure in eating, it may be useful to recall that many have found it helpful to become more involved in both cooking their meals from the basic ingredients and growing their own vegetables, even in the smallest of urban gardens. This may mean pulling up a few slabs and sowing a few seeds, or buying a cookbook and measuring scales. It is the testimony of countless newborn cooks and gardeners that such processes are healing and certainly make us stop and think and be more grateful about our food and relate more positively with the rest of creation. Such actions also benefit the land; through lifting slabs and planting, various life-forms are attracted where they previously had not been. It can also save air miles through not needing so much imported food. This further means we save oil, processing costs, and packaging.

When I began growing some of my own food in our garden, it transformed both the cooking and the eating of what my family ate. I recognized that the tomato I was cooking and eating was sown in April as a tiny seed, and now by some magic and tireless watering and weeding, it became a delicious tomato. Gardening has sensitized me to Jesus's teachings about praying for our food.

In sum, when we pray, "Give us today our daily bread," there are profound ecological implications calling us to change our lifestyles so that we can become in tune with the words.

Release Our Debts

I am influenced by Sharon Ringe's suggestion that the language and imagery of the petition "Release our debts" are associated with Jubilee traditions.[6] The Greek word often translated "sins" in the Lord's Prayer usually means debts, while the word rendered "forgive" often suggests "release." "Debt" and "release" together usually refer to an economic or legal obligation; therefore, the petition concerns the release of debts in an economic way.[7]

Ringe's interpretation is further supported by the fact that a major aspect of God's re-creating actions in human history has meant releasing those suffering from economic and political oppression. Jesus calls his disciples to practice compassion through giving: "Give to everyone who begs from you, and do not refuse anyone who wants to borrow from you" (Matthew 5:42).

Therefore, for the disempowered and humiliated, freedom meant release from literal oppression when others shared their natural resources; for example, sharing land or clearing debts. What about those disciples who do not suffer from lack of resources? Being released for them is recognizing the nature of their sin, that is, that they actually have something to be released from. When sinners are released from their sin, they act mercifully to redress the consequences of their sins, such as by giving land to the hungry and canceling the debts of those who have nothing. In so acting they are also released from the stress and hardship of being enslaved by their property and the fear of losing it. Zacchaeus is a good example of one who experiences liberation from his debts to God when he releases others from their material debts by giving his wealth to those he had previously robbed (Luke 19:8).

Jesus is calling those who follow him to live generously. Generous giving frees the poor from their enslavement to terrible poverty, as well as freeing disciples from their own slavery to wealth and security.

We should also recall Jesus's teaching about the merciless servant as a description of how people should *not* act (Matthew 18:23–35). In the parable, a servant owes the king more than can be repaid but is released from all his debts out of the king's compassion. Alas, however, the same servant when seeing his fellow servant who owes him money says, "Give me what you owe" (see Matthew 18:28). Unfortunately, he does not release his fellow servant from the small debt he owed in the same way he had been released from his large debt by the king. Instead, the unforgiving servant has his fellow servant imprisoned until he pays his debts (Matthew 18:30). For this the previously forgiven servant is condemned (Matthew 18:34).

Ecological Significance. If we ask God to "release our debts" without seeking justice for all, we are babblers heaping up empty words (Matthew 6:7–8). To pray this petition meaningfully, we must cultivate a sense of gratitude for the things we have; maybe the food on our plate or the garden that we are able to cultivate. We must recognize that we are recipients of God's mercy and forgiveness and therefore are to show mercy ourselves. We recognize that God has given much to us and that we too must give.

Echlin offers some specific ecological implications of the Lord's Prayer and its emphasis on "forgiving":

> Penance, unction and our penitential prayers should include personal structural ecological sins with which we, as a counter-cultural people, cannot co-operate: questionable arms and tobacco trade, unnecessary construction, socially and environmentally damaging tourism, and the manipulative media, whether religious or secular, none of which we have adequately changed. When we "call to mind our sins," therefore let us include our own participation in structural ecological sin.[8]

In asking God to forgive us our sins, we acknowledge the sin itself, and therefore we repent. Much we have in the West has involved both environmental damage and social oppression as Echlin observes above. In the last chapter we saw the damage caused by our need for oil. We can repent by lightening our touch on the earth through more restrained and careful living. This petition involves us in asking what harm our lives have on others.

Therefore, like Zacchaeus, we must repent, emphatically thinking of our "structural ecological sin." We might, for example, think more carefully about driving our cars one mile when we could walk or ride a bicycle. Saying this petition of the Lord's Prayer must go alongside consuming things that cause less harm to others whether that is human, plant, or animal. We must not be like the unforgiving servant, who has been forgiven but chooses to ignore the king's mercy by treating others harshly.

Temptation and Evil

Jesus acknowledges that humanity can be led into the power of the evil one through temptation, especially temptation associated with suffering, which can lead humans to disobey and curse God and thus become servants of evil. Jesus himself had struggled with temptation associated with suffering in the wilderness and throughout his ministry. But despite this he trusted God and was thus delivered from evil.

Jesus experienced great temptation on account of his suffering in the wilderness. At the heart of the Devil's modus operandi was to lead Jesus to be tempted by worldly success. This is reflected in the three temptations Jesus experienced but that the Gospels make clear he did not succumb to, either in the wilderness or in his ministry.

Similarly, Jesus, while waiting in Gethsemane to be delivered into the hands of Judas and the authorities, prayed to avoid the sufferings of humiliation, beatings, betrayal, and painful death that he knew were about to come upon him (Matthew 26:39). But the narrative tells us that Jesus did not give in and flee from the suffering that his faithfulness to God was leading him toward. Jesus was tempted but was not delivered into the hands of evil.

Jesus is also tempted by Peter (Matthew 16:23). Peter wants success, and this desire leads him to evil and to doubt Jesus's understanding of God's way. We find in Matthew 16:26 Jesus instructing his disciples: "For what will it profit them if they gain the whole world but forfeit their life? Or what will they give in return for their life?" Jesus teaches how mad it is to give one's life to gain profit in money and success. The nature of temptation is to lead people to want these things. Carter writes, "To invest oneself in maintaining or increasing power, wealth, and status, even to the point of owning the world, is loss because it is not the means of participating in God's purposes now or in the eschaton."[9]

In the Lord's Prayer, Jesus urges his disciples to pray to be delivered from the evil one. We must observe that Jesus doesn't teach his disciples to pray to be delivered from temptation or suffering. They are to pray to their heavenly Father to have the strength to face the temptations and sufferings that lead to distrusting God. Jesus teaches his disciples to acknowledge their inability to resist the evil one and thereby rely on God.

The disciples in following Jesus reject the way of the world with its temptations to remove suffering by succumbing to greed and self-interest. The disciples in following Jesus would indeed face temptation because they would expect suffering through confronting a world that hated Jesus. This is what Jesus means when he says, "If any want to become my followers, let them deny themselves and take up their cross and follow me" (Matthew 16:24). Jesus is saying that God will lead the faithful through times of temptation so that healing to the world can occur through faithfulness. We pray, "Deliver us from evil," believing that our addiction to material wealth, comfort, and success will become less powerful. This will enable us to withstand temptation to conform to a society that pursues greed and self-interest. Instead, we remain firm in the vision of hope of God's goal of cosmic justice.

It would have been so easy for the disciples to leave Jesus and return to their work as fishermen and tax collectors, especially when the road got difficult. Those who don't give up also can be led into that utter sense of hopelessness that Jesus experienced in Gethsemane (Matthew 26:38–39). In the garden, Jesus says to Peter, "Pray that you may not come into the time of trial; the spirit indeed is willing, but the flesh is weak" (Matthew 26:41). Peter is told to pray that he may withstand the temptation to doubt God's faithfulness and his own commitment to do God's will. Many of us who have read biographies of those who have stood out against injustice or oppression know that such people often face doubts about what they are doing.

Jesus's words to Peter in Gethsemane and on the mount to his disciples assume that humanity cannot avoid temptation to doubt God's will. The disciples are tempted, but Jesus instructs them to rely on God for deliverance from the temptations and tests that come their way and so continue proclaiming the good news of release and healing despite hardship.[10] Disciples must pray for the strength to stay on the right road that brings life, even though there are constant temptations to return to the old habits that can lead to evil, such as engaging in activities that satisfy our greed and make us feel part of the world, for instance careless eating, drinking, shopping, and entertainment.

Ecological Significance. As Christians we all face temptations in modern society. We encounter them through viewing advertising and media, consulting image gurus, looking good, having a nice car, and many more activities generally involving consuming. If we are honest, very few of us remain unaffected by consumer materialism with its promise of happiness and contentment.

We are also imaginative at justifying why we can't cut back and use our money to help release the afflicted from their suffering or support ventures to encourage fairer distribution of God's creation. We find it easy to argue that having a big car makes life easier and safer for our family while ignoring the pollution that it causes, as well as using up our decreasing oil resources.

We are brought up with habits of consumption that are far from God's way. They are contrary to his way because they lead to our own suffering, the suffering of the human community, as well as suffering and death of animals, plants, and the whole planet.

So we must pray and act to be aware of the suffering our consuming causes. When we pray, "Lead us not into temptation, but deliver us from evil," we are asking God to encourage us and to support us in our practice of careful consumption. We must pray to our Lord Jesus to help us cultivate the soil in a sustainable manner, rather than supporting soil erosion through consuming things that demand intensive factory farming. We must ask Jesus to be with us when shopping at the market so that we buy the vegetables and fruits that are cultivated sustainably. Perhaps when we fill our car with gas, we thank God for the earth that has produced this oil and pledge to use it more responsibly.

Chapter Summary

Jesus teaches his disciples that they must cancel anything that puts another in their power. It is likely that Jesus is teaching his followers to cancel each other's debts, as well as not holding personal grudges. Jesus's petition is elucidated by the story of rich Zacchaeus and the parable of the unforgiving servant. These stories place the idea of "forgiving sins" in the context of God's reign, the onset of which is marked by forgiveness and release from the patterns of debts and obligation by which the old order is maintained.[11]

Jesus teaches his disciples to pray for bread necessary for the day. Food is the stuff of creation and God's gift. It is also evidence of human dependency on the rest of creation. In praying for food, we align ourselves with a community that values all creation for its intrinsic value to God. In response to this, we are called to show carefulness in the way we purchase, consume, and share.

In following Jesus and taking up our cross and embracing the suffering that entails, we should expect temptation to doubt the worth and value of God's way. In our economically developed nations we must pray increasingly for the courage to face up to the trials ahead brought about by living godly lives: giving more money to projects that support the environment; living more economically; standing out for ecological justice where it is not popular; cycling rather than driving; avoiding fast food; participating in activities that seek to renew open spaces for growing, and so on. We must pray for each other as we support each other in our tasks of caring and transforming this world into the one God desires.

Reflection Questions

1. When we pray these three petitions, how can we embody them in our practical lives?
2. Most of us have more choices of food than we could possibly want; can we pray, "Give us our daily bread," given these choices?
3. What temptations might lead you to give up on God's vision of cosmic justice?

Chapter 10

FOOD MAKES THE WORLD GO ROUND

The author of Proverbs 4 defines the unjust as those who "eat the bread of wickedness" (Proverbs 4:17). In another proverb it is written, "Better is a dinner of vegetables where love is than a fatted ox and hatred with it" (Proverbs 15:17). How and what we eat says a lot about our health, as well as our attitudes toward others and the rest of creation.

For a long time, I've been under the misunderstanding that if I don't spend most of my time making money I will have no quality of life. We who live in North America or Europe need lots of money, and if we don't have money, our lives are perceived as "unsuccessful." Therefore, we work harder, becoming stressed, anxious, sick, incapable of sleep, and then depressed—all because we think we need lots of money.

In 2007 I spent five months at St Philip's Theological College in rural Tanzania, where I found a way of life that was much simpler, and I began to wonder how much I "needed" to be satisfied. I decided much less than I had previously thought. This led me to try to live on less money when I returned to the UK. We got rid of our car, started growing more of our own vegetables, spent less on luxuries such as books, a new television, and new clothes, took holidays within a couple hundred kilometers of our home, and generally tried to consume less.

In growing our own vegetables, I realized how much money we spent on food and how much money we were saving by growing our own. I am not saying that we are self-sufficient, but my wife and I certainly rejoice at not having to go to the supermarket as often as we did. We of course have to make money, but I believe we must ask ourselves how much money we really need and how many extra hours of work to pay for things we can do without.

This chapter is devoted to food and the New Testament. We find that the central concern of Jesus's instruction is to preach and embody the coming of the kingdom of God in his life and teachings. This kingdom is the reign of God on earth for all creation. It is, therefore, not surprising that food plays a significant part in Jesus's descriptions of the kingdom of God. The coming of God's reign involves humans seeing their relationship with the rest of earth more harmoniously and not something that humans fight over. We have much to learn from the New Testament about food.

Thinking about Food

Food is the most obvious and intimate connection between humans and the earth. By seeking to understand our relationship with food, we must also consider our relationship with all creation. Jesus's teachings leave us with a view that food is a wonderful gift and that we must eat thankfully, carefully, understanding the story behind the food we consume.

Food is the basis of society; how we eat directly impinges on our world; therefore, it follows that making food and drink a primary focus for Christian witness is vital. We can't exist without food and drink, and without food and drink money would be meaningless. For countless generations people on small farms have existed by cultivating the soil to feed the family. A hard life, but life is hardly easy today. We are becoming increasingly de-skilled, unfit, and addicted to making money in order to have the things that are not always healthy or good for us. We are in a circle of madness that leads to unhealthy lives.

Our way with food leads to starvation, inequality, cruelty to animals, the loss of family farms, and food-related conditions such as obesity. Bulimia and anorexia appear, causing much suffering and also indicating that society has lost its positive connection to food. We eat and drink from plastic plates and Styrofoam cups off artificial surfaces all created by chemists. We eat food grown by impersonal agribusiness, which is sold merely as a commodity. We are unmindful of the superior quality of food exported to us from poor countries while their inhabitants eat inferior foods.

Do we know that 95 percent of the food we eat today is oil dependent? Do we know that each year 4.6 million hectares of tropical rain forests are destroyed to make way for agriculture to satisfy the huge appetites of developed nations? Do we know that food and agriculture account for an estimated one-third of global greenhouse gas emissions? Do we know that "current food systems" are, according to Carolyn Steel in the *Ecologist*, so destructive there is little chance of them lasting another forty years?[1]

Table Fellowship in the Gospels

The Gospels show that sharing food with others was at the heart of Jesus's ministry. Jesus challenged views that saw table fellowship as a way of maintaining a status quo of political, social, economic, and religious hierarchy. I believe, therefore, that Jesus's table fellowship should be understood as a vehicle of cultural protest, challenging the ethos and politics of holiness, pointing to an inclusive community reflecting the compassion of God. Jesus's table fellowship is so important that Paul, James, and John in Revelation are particularly critical of the way some, to whom they wrote, were not following the example of Jesus and were using food as a way of being separate from others. There can be little doubt that food was central to Jesus's ministry and teaching.

Jesus ate with all kinds of people: the rich, the Pharisees, the sick, the disabled, the disciples, large crowds, and women. He was inclusive and embracing rather than exclusive and excluding. Eating with another was an expression of intimacy and fellowship; to invite people to a meal honored them and expressed both trust and acceptance.[2] This is particularly significant when we consider that in the ancient world meal customs reflected and reinforced hierarchical order; the type of food that was given to a guest reflected the guest's standing in society. Pliny the Younger describes the host giving to himself and a small number of eminent friends the best food with the rest given poorer quality foods.[3]

When Jesus ate with the defiled and those in league with Rome, that is, tax collectors, he was suspected of denying his own people as he appeared to accept and thereby forgive Israel's enemies. Therefore, Jesus exemplifies in his table fellowship the way of embrace.

Luke recounts how the embracing nature of table fellowship effects healing. Jesus's table fellowship with Zacchaeus (Luke 19:1–10), the extorter of the Jewish people, leads him to change his lifestyle, to live no longer for money, but to restore what he has plundered, with interest. Jesus does not say to Zacchaeus, "If you will guarantee to return to the poor all you took I will come to eat with you."[4] Rather, Jesus accepts him and so brings about Zacchaeus's repentance. Jesus's eating with sinners and tax collectors was not connivance with evil, but a way of shaming, humbling, and converting it, by love and not by force.[5]

Jesus is also critical of hospitality customs. In Luke 14:7–14, Jesus observes how the guests chose places of honor at the dinner table (v. 7). On the basis of his observation of such elitism, he said:

> When you give a luncheon or a dinner, do not invite your friends or your brothers or your relatives or rich neighbors, in case they may invite you in return, and you would be repaid. But when you give a banquet, invite the poor, the crippled, the lame, and the blind. And you will be blessed, because they cannot repay you, for you will be repaid at the resurrection of the righteous. (Luke 14:12–14)

These verses suggest how alternative Jesus's teaching was and how difficult to put into practice. Jesus teaches that those who "have" should give without expecting anything back in return; for what they are given is not theirs but God's. To invite guests with the expectation of receiving back assumes that there is no generosity but just a way of sustaining the status quo. Jesus's observations and teachings on dinner etiquette are thus the opposite of the usual, where things are shared among social equals.

It is not, therefore, surprising that Jesus is challenged by the Pharisees as to why he eats and drinks with tax collectors and sinners (Matthew 9:11). Jesus's response is revealing: "Go and learn what this means, 'I desire mercy, not sacrifice'" (Matthew 9:13).

Jesus tells them that seeking mercy is seeking God's justice; this challenges the exclusionary practices and structures of the elite and seeks to establish a life-giving community of shared resources that sustains and builds relationships rather than dividing and excluding.

In sum, Jesus in his table fellowship represents a way of challenging a world where the abundance of God's creation is mistreated and manipulated for the use of the elite. Bread and wine are central in Jesus's actions, and in sharing food and drink with those considered unholy, he shows his acceptance and love for them. He shares with them the very essence of creation that God has intended for humans to enjoy and share regardless of culture or economic class or, for that matter, species.

Plucking Grain on the Sabbath

The disciples' action of plucking grain on the Sabbath fits with what we know of Jesus's teaching about table fellowship, as well as Jesus's concern for the hungry. Matthew writes, "At that time Jesus went through the grainfields on the sabbath; his disciples were hungry, and they began to pluck heads of grain and to eat. When the Pharisees saw it, they said to him, 'Look, your disciples are doing what is not lawful to do on the sabbath'" (12:1–2).

The disciples are hungry, and on the Sabbath they pluck heads of grain to eat. Grain was a basic resource, and hunger and food shortages were not unusual because of weather, human hoarding, profiteering, and war. The hardest hit were not the wealthy, but, as would be expected, the poor. Writing in a time of high prices and food shortages, this point is illustrated by Gaius Petronius, adviser to the Roman emperor Nero, who records a comment that the "jaws of the upper classes" do well while "the little people come off badly."[6]

Matthew records that Jesus's disciples were plucking grain on the Sabbath. The Sabbath is the day Israel celebrated its deliverance from Egypt (Deuteronomy 5:12–15) and is first mentioned in Scripture in connection with the food God supplies in the wilderness (Exodus 16:16–30). The Sabbath evokes hopeful visions of cosmic justice, recognizing God's liberating work and his provision of food. The Sabbath also recalls creation and anticipates God's re-creating work. We have already seen that the Sabbath is linked to the Jubilee laws. On the Sabbath, God's people are to rest and recognize and celebrate his reign over the world (Exodus 20:8–11; for the negative, see Isaiah 1:13). That reign was further recognized in a Sabbath year every seven years. This year meant rest for the land, food for the poor, freedom for slaves, and release from debt. The Jubilee every fifty years meant the return of property and land to their original holders. In sum, the Sabbath is that which humanity looks to for the restoration and establishment of cosmic justice.

In the light of this dual background of "grain" and "Sabbath," Carter comments, "In this scene Jesus resists controls on the Sabbath which harm the poor by limiting access to food resources."[7] The idea of linking the Sabbath to that of denying access to food is a contradiction in terms. Food is central to Jesus's ministry of challenging a society that keeps the poor without, and the Sabbath provides the day on which we envisage God's completion of creation.

From Jesus's perspective, "every plant yielding seed that is upon the face of all the earth, and every tree with seed in its fruit" are potential food (Genesis 1:29). However, through ownership, indebtedness, taxes, and tolls, God's intentions had been thwarted, and land and food were now the basis of a culture where the rich stayed rich and the poor stayed poor. Jesus challenges the Pharisees for restricting access to food resources on the Sabbath (Matthew 12:3–8). He reminds them how on the Sabbath it was permitted for the hungry to eat (Matthew 12:3–4).

As long as there was hunger, the Sabbath was not being obeyed, nor was its vision of cosmic justice understood. Carter writes, "He [Jesus] argues that the sabbath praxis should be shaped by the merciful divine mandate to meet basic needs."[8] Jesus further quotes Hosea 6:6: "I desire mercy and not sacrifice." In so doing Jesus says mercy is not pity but doing God's justice, which challenges the restrictive practices and structures of the status quo and seeks to establish a life-giving community of shared resources.[9]

In sum, Jesus's response to the Pharisees regarding his disciples plucking grain does not reject the Sabbath. Jesus teaches a merciful and life-giving way, which is what the Sabbath anticipates.

Feeding of the Hungry

Jesus's table fellowship and his response to plucking grain on the Sabbath show his concern for the hungry. The Gospels document Jesus's feeding of five thousand and four thousand hungry followers in two separate events (Matthew 14:13–20 and 15:32–39; Mark 6:30–44 and 8:1–10). In these narratives food is central to Jesus's ministry in terms of his concern to feed the hungry and to show the value of food and the importance of sharing it with one another. The two accounts in Matthew and Mark are very similar, so why are they both included? Richard France observes particularly in reference to Matthew that "this second feeding follows from two accounts of Jesus's ministry to Gentiles, and apparently involves the same Gentile crowd who have just 'glorified the God of Israel' (v. 31), suggest that we have here a deliberate indication that the benefits given to Israel by their Messiah were also to be available outside the Jewish circle."[10]

Carter argues that Jesus's actions in feeding the hungry attack the injustice of the sinful system that ensures that the urban elite are well fed at the expense of the poor.[11] His actions embody an alternative system marked by generosity and shared resources as he also taught in the Beatitudes.

Carter's argument is supported insofar as Matthew places the account of the feeding of the five thousand alongside a description of King Herod's extravagant and hedonistic banquet in Matthew 14:1–12. On Herod's birthday, only the elite were invited to his banquet. Here also the outcome was the beheading of John the Baptist. In contrast, the outcome of Jesus's acts of feeding is well-being and equality. The hunger of the large crowd Jesus faces is real hunger just as that of the disciples when they plucked the grain on the Sabbath. The feeding miracle is, therefore, in part a demand for economic and social justice.

I believe that the feeding miracle stories invite readers to friendship and relationship with one another. Jesus's feeding of the five thousand breaks the norm of eating only among your social grouping. This is seen even more in Matthew's and Mark's second account of the feeding of the four thousand in a Gentile area (Matthew 15:32–39; Mark 8:1–10). In this account the disciples don't show concern for the four thousand as they did with the five thousand. Instead, Jesus tells them to feed them, whereas in the story of the feeding of the five thousand, the disciples made the initial move in providing food for the hungry crowd. This may be because the four thousand were not Jews but Gentiles. So Jesus is crossing cultural boundaries, as well as responding to real need.

We should also not miss that the Gospels tell us that the disciples gathered up what food was left over, stating that at the end of the feeding of the five thousand, there was enough fragments of food to fill twelve baskets (Matthew 14:20), and in the feeding of the four thousand, there were seven baskets (Matthew 15:37). Such tells us that Jesus is able to provide more than our needs. In John's feeding account in 6:12, Jesus orders the disciples to gather up what is left over. I suggest that this be read as demonstrating good ecological sense. He does not allow any food to be wasted, nor does he allow the hillside to be trashed with garbage. Those scraps that might otherwise be trampled underfoot, or left on the ground to rot, are carefully and purposefully preserved.

Jesus's feeding of the crowd also demonstrates that God's re-creating activities involve not just humans but all creation. In feeding the crowd, Jesus gave thanks for the bread and fish before giving them to his disciples to distribute (Matthew 14:19 and 15:36). In giving thanks, he values God as Creator of all that is good.

The feeding of the five thousand and four thousand anticipates God's re-created order, where his reign is established in full and where there will be abundance of food for all. Jesus's actions demonstrate God's sovereignty over creation, that it is God who provides and no other. The health of humans depends on the health of all creation.

Therefore, the feeding narratives provide another example of the centrality of creation as belonging to God and him caring for it. Humans are not to hoard, worry about, or fight for food. To do so is to treat God's creation with contempt, for such human actions are carried out as though humanity has the right to use creation for self-interest. Instead, humanity is to trust God by obeying his commandments, which call for mercy and compassion.

In sum, Jesus's actions critique the practices that had led to hunger. They also anticipate God's reign, where all will eat together, sharing, delighting, and, most importantly, rejoicing in the abundance of his extravagant generosity.

Summary. The accounts of feeding the hungry anticipate the kingdom of God when there will be no hunger and where there will be abundance for all as long as people trust God by actually seeking his cosmic justice. To seek cosmic justice is to live generously. Jesus in feeding the five thousand and four thousand embodies his own teaching of care for all creation recounted in the Beatitudes.

The feeding narratives also give us a glimpse of God's kingdom in contrast to humanity's kingdom. Herod's banquet shows extravagance and greed. In contrast, God's kingdom is one where all people who are hungry will be fed when they trust him.

Trusting God is not waiting with "open hands," begging, but working and caring for the land based on the economics of sharing within community. Overall, Jesus demonstrated that the world is filled with abundance. If bread is shared, there is enough for all.

The Last Supper

Jesus's Last Supper must be read in the same light as his table fellowship, the plucking of the grain, and the feeding of the multitudes. I will focus my attention on Matthew's account in chapter 26:

> Jesus took a loaf of bread, and after blessing it he broke it, gave it to the disciples, and said, "Take, eat; this is my body." Then he took a cup, and after giving thanks he gave it to them, saying, "Drink from it, all of you; for this is my blood of the covenant, which is poured out for many for the forgiveness of sins. I tell you, I will never again drink of this fruit of the vine until that day when I drink it new with you in my Father's kingdom." (vv. 26–29)

Jesus's blessing of the bread and giving thanks for the wine demonstrate that food is a gift from God as is all creation.[12] Echlin emphasizes that "the whole earth community is included in bread and wine as it is in our bodies."[13] Therefore, Jesus's blessing and giving thanks demonstrate that creation matters to God; through the Eucharist creation is celebrated as God's work.

The Eucharist is an ecological sacrament because it is a sign of the God-given character of all creation and not just of humanity. Blessing and giving thanks reiterate the centrality of Jesus's belief in God as the good Creator who provides for all. The Eucharist is that special time when we can recollect specifically this ecological wisdom that we should embody in all our daily activities.

Davies and Allison make the connection between the Eucharist and the earth more explicit. They observe that the "blessing" of the bread and wine alludes to a traditional formula: "Blessed are thou, O Lord our God, king of the universe, who bringest forth bread from the earth."[14] Similarly, Echlin writes:

> The Eucharist makes us peacemakers, for militarism destroys the fields where grain and grapes grow and the children who are always wars' losers, whether living today or tomorrow. We can beat offensive weapons into sustainable

hospitals, schools, housing, orchards, wheat fields and habitats.[15]

If we acknowledge that it is God who brings bread from the earth, then we in giving thanks in the Eucharist cannot at the same time easily and consciously ignore the story of our food and the suffering caused by its production. To treat food with contempt is to be noneucharistic.

In Jesus's act of breaking the bread, he is also telling his disciples, "Let the breaking and sharing of your continued fellowship remind you of how my life was broken and poured out for God's purposes of salvation, and may you do likewise."[16] The "breaking of the bread" signifies the Messiah's broken body.[17] Jesus, like the rest of God's creation, is plundered, rejected, tortured, and brutally murdered. Jesus in comparing himself to bread and wine reveals to humanity how it plunders what is important to God.

In feasting on Jesus, the disciples know that he reveals God's vision, which is true nourishment and joy for all. In feeding on the bread and wine, the body and blood of Jesus, the disciples make his story their story, his teaching their teaching, his vision their vision, his death their death, and his resurrection their resurrection. So in partaking of the eucharistic bread and wine, we are aligning ourselves to Jesus, which means to take up the cross and follow him.

At the Last Supper, Jesus pours out his life "for the release of sins." As we have already seen, "forgiveness" or "release" suggests that the Jubilee year is being alluded to. To read this as simply having one's personal relationship with God restored does not do full justice to the text, although this clearly is part of the release. Jesus is broken because he stood out against the injustices that resulted in the afflictions of many people. Jesus is speaking here of the good news of release and healing of the poor and afflicted, as well as the transformation of the wealthier who seek to work for the release of the afflicted. He himself says that he is the anointed one to proclaim liberty/release to the captives, good news to the oppressed, to bind up the brokenhearted (Isaiah 61:1–2 and Luke 4:18–19). Release from sins, then, has personal and sociopolitical, cosmic, and present and future dimensions.[18] We will explore more how Jesus's death results in such release when we consider the resurrection hope later in this chapter.

At the Last Supper, Jesus also states that he will not drink of the vine again until he is in his Father's kingdom. Here we read of the anticipation of the future establishment of God's reign on earth involving food and drink.

Food in Paul's Letters

Paul sums up his view on food: "So, whether you eat or drink, or whatever you do, do everything for the glory of God" (1 Corinthians 10:31). Eating and drinking can bring glory to God but can also bring dishonor on God's name.

Paul is concerned with what some were eating. He writes, "You cannot drink the cup of the Lord and the cup of demons. You cannot partake of the table of the Lord and the table of demons" (1 Corinthians 10:21). Paul says that the Corinthians cannot partake of food that is thought to be inconsistent with God, something that is offered to idols, which is akin to worshiping demons, which are not God. How you eat, with whom you eat, and what you eat suggest where your alliances are.

Despite Paul's language of demons and idols, we should not be distracted from the issue of meals being political and economic. Eating and drinking are political and economic actions insofar as to eat and drink at the table with those treating the meal like that of a Roman symposium is to identify with elitism, greed, and idolatry. Paul counsels Christians to desist from eating meat in Corinth because such meat was offered to idols as a form of worship of demons (1 Corinthians 10:20). For Paul, by eating such meat, Christians risked becoming embedded in an idolatrous and pagan worldview where Caesar was Lord. In practice this meant supporting the Roman economy that was rooted in hierarchy, oppression, and hoarding, while Paul called for sharing as practiced by Jesus in his table fellowship[19] and at the Last Supper.

Paul tells the Corinthian Christians that they should not seek their own advantage but that of the other (1 Corinthians 10:24) and that they should act in a way that honors God. But Paul saw that the table fellowship in Corinth was at odds with Jesus's example and teaching. Paul saw that the rich Corinthian Christians were hoarding and excluding the poor from table fellowship (1 Corinthians 11:17–22). They were doing something that was the very opposite of what Jesus had commanded his disciples to do,[20] which was to care for and seek the advantage of the other. These rich Corinthians were also in opposition to the two rules that Israel should have learned from its time in the wilderness and that both Jew and Gentile Christians would have known. From the story of Israel's sojourn in the wilderness, it learned that (1) people should eat only what is sufficient and that (2) they should not hoard.[21]

In sum, to use food as a way of excluding others is a clear example of not honoring God and degrades his creation by preventing it being as he intended. Therefore eating and partaking in meals that were dedicated to supporting Roman elitism was seen as contrary to Jesus's table fellowship.

Food in the Epistle of James

Like Paul, James attacks church practices regarding meals where the meals are opportunities for the rich to eat first and have their fill of luxury foods, while the servants cleaned up and ate the leftovers when the wealthy were done.[22] On the contrary, the practice of sharing through table fellowship as Jesus taught and exemplified was not being practiced. James tells his readers they must put their trust in God: "Yet you do not even know what tomorrow will bring. What is your life? For you are a mist that appears for a little while and then vanishes. Instead you ought to say, 'If the Lord wishes, we will live and do this or that'" (James 4:14–15). James particularly emphasizes trusting God for his bounty mentioning the rain and the earth itself which together yield its harvest (James 5:17).

It seems that the church James addresses was showing favoritism, particularly in regard to where the rich sit, that is, in the best places presumably getting the best food, thus openly showing disdain for God (James 2:1–4). James rebukes this practice and further challenges ordinary Christians who ignore their brothers and sisters who are naked and lack daily food while honoring the rich who persecute the poor (James 2:15). James insists that their faith in Christ must be demonstrated in supplying the daily and bodily needs of the poor. He condemns the rich who are living in luxury and holding back the goodness of creation to others so that they might have more (James 4:13). James says of them, "On earth you have had a life of comfort and luxury; in the time of slaughter you went on eating to your heart's content" (James 5:5 NJB).

In sum, James attacks a system of greed and self-interest that he saw occurring in the church. He rebuked the hypocrisy of those who professed faith but who practiced holding back from others what was due (5:4), seeing their meals as more akin to meals that served to perpetuate inequality and elitism. As Northcott observes, that which sets apart Christian times of eating from pagan meals is "that the food offered and consumed was seen as the gift of God, Creator of the universe."[23] This is what James envisaged.

Food in Revelation 2:14, 20

We will look in more detail at the book of Revelation in chapter 13. My concern here is to emphasize that the book of Revelation makes it very clear that all creation belongs to God (Revelation 4:11; 5:13). Further, it states that God is praised for "destroying those who destroy the earth" (Revelation 11:18).

Revelation was written in the late 90s during the reign of Domitian. Its author, known as John, was concerned at how Rome with its promise of wealth and gain was drawing Christians to compromise with it, even through participating in worship of the emperor. Revelation 2:14 and 20 challenge Christians in the imperial cities of Pergamum and Thyatira for eating food sacrificed to idols. To participate in eating such food is to participate in everything Rome stood for. Rome claimed for itself divine authority over the world. In reality it was a system of violent oppression, founded on conquest, maintained by violence and oppression, including economic oppression.[24] Ultimately, to compromise with

Rome meant denying that God is Creator and that God cares for his creation.

Nelson Kraybill has shown that Rome's economy was based on greed, self-aggrandizement, and power.[25] Even Seneca, Nero's court philosopher, was appalled by Roman consumption run riot.[26] In Revelation, Rome is also depicted as one who brings plagues and pollution upon nonhuman creation (Revelation 6; 8:6–9:19; 11:15–18; 16).

Bauckham comments that those who were eating food sacrificed to idols were teaching that it was possible for Christians to be successful in pagan society.[27] Like others in the Roman Empire, they would hoard and oppress others so that they were not able to eat. They would become "destroyers of the earth" (Revelation 11:18 RSV). They are also idolaters who reject that creation belongs to God—they plunder the earth for their own benefit. Rome has taken the best foods, drinks, and spices from the provinces (Revelation 18:13) and is condemned for it: "For in one hour all this wealth has been laid waste!" (Revelation 18:17).

Ecological Significance

In light of the evidence of brokenness revealed in the growing gap between rich and poor, as well as the human failure to address issues relating to the ecological crisis, we cannot be despondent as Christians. The hope of Jesus's resurrection inspires us in the present to live as Jesus did, caring for all. Hope for the universal divine transformation of all reality should lead the faithful to a world based on God's justice. However, such striving will mean that the faithful are unreconciled to the present condition, "a constant disturbance in human society."[28]

Food That Contains Suffering

Like some of the original readers of the New Testament, we don't want to know the truth about the food on our table, as seems to be the case among those whom Paul, James, and John in Revelation address. Will Tuttle puts it well:

> We were all born into a culture that forces us, virtually from birth, to eat the flesh and secretions of certain animals who are bred, confined and killed for this purpose. Early on, we are taught the habit of disconnecting the reality that is on our plate from the reality of getting it on our plate. We become masters of the art of disconnection.[29]

At eucharistic worship when we see the bread being broken, we are called to see how we harm the soil, air, rivers, and all forms of life on earth. We must think carefully about the various processes food has gone through: Who has been involved? How far it has traveled? How much oil has been used in its production? In doing so we recall to what extent our way of eating involves manipulation and exclusion. Unrestrained and unmindful consumption means that only a few get to have table fellowship.

On many occasions in our lives we will eat and drink something that has caused suffering both socially and environmentally. Therefore, when we look at the full plate of food in front of us, we should be aware of the bitter pain and suffering of people and the rest of creation because we can eat. We who live in North America or Europe expect top-quality, imported foods such as coffee and chocolate and year-round supplies of otherwise seasonal fruit and vegetables. As we eat, we must recall that children in these producing countries, except those from rich families, may never see such fine products. They eat inferior foods. The finer foods we eat are put aside for us in order to provide foreign exchange. I remember being surprised at not being able to purchase good-quality coffee when arriving in Tanzania because it was all being exported to North America and Europe.

Valuing Our Need for Creation

In sharing food we must constantly recall that the food we eat is evidence of our need for the whole of creation, which supports our existence. In sharing our food with others, we celebrate God as Creator, in whom we must trust. In eating carefully we allow God's whole creation to bear rich fruit and in so doing allow the whole of creation to praise

God in doing what he has intended for it. As humans we are to care by bringing what God has made to fulfill its potential.

One terrible and glaring example of the way we devalue God's creation is by wasting food. We have seen how after Jesus had fed the crowds, the disciples carefully collected what was left over rather than throwing it away. I believe this should inspire us to do the same. I have often been struck by the carefulness of some priests and ministers who do not waste any of the consecrated bread and wine in the eucharistic service. While waste might not always be the primary concern of those officiating at the Eucharist, I certainly think it should be a consideration. Waste is a huge ecological issue. John Lane highlights the issue of waste in our world:

> The wastage of food in the USA is extreme: one hundred billion pounds of it goes to waste every year. Much of it seems to be left on plates in public restaurants. Nonetheless, statistics show that over 50 per cent of all adults in the US are overweight, and almost 25 per cent are clinically obese. On any given day, half of American women and one in four men are on a diet. Yet according to *Forum News Daily*, 31 million people in the world are hungry or at risk of hunger.
>
> In a typical week, Wal-Mart serves 70 million customers with packaged produce: eggs in cartons, drinks in cans, fizzy lemonade in plastic bottles, frozen food wrapped in cardboard and cellophane. On average, Americans discard 1,455 pounds of garbage every year. Every day the city of New York has to dispose of 24,000 tonnes of trash.[30]

Table Fellowship and Discipleship

Table fellowship is a helpful metaphor for thinking about "discipleship." Disciples must look at hunger in our world and respond to it by actions coherent with what table fellowship represents. How can disciples today be true to Jesus's teachings about table fellowship? Human populations are increasing, and there is a greater demand for food. Land, rivers, and seas are becoming polluted, and flooding and loss of arable land are predicted.

Jesus's table fellowship is a call to mindfulness as we use the eating of bread as a way of recalling the suffering of others. Table fellowship represents more than actually sitting down and eating; it represents the need to discern that the most essential activity befitting humans is to secure the food system that God gives to sustain all creatures whatever their species, culture, or class.

We must imaginatively seek opportunities to share God's creation with those who are denied it. We live in a noneucharistic world (a non-thankful world), where a small percentage of the world's population controls who gets what. Therefore, either in the more formal setting of eucharistic worship or in sharing food with others or in growing our own food, we should recall that as we offer up bread (food) and wine (drink), we are giving thanks, thereby repeating Jesus's actions of offering thanks and therefore affirming the goodness of creation. Leech comments that to participate in the Eucharist is to engage in a socially, ecologically, politically, and economically subversive act.[31] As we gather to enact Jesus's Last Supper, we are to share food with the dispossessed. In doing so we are withdrawing from a system that controls the earth's resources for self-interest.

Therefore, the table fellowship of the Eucharist should call us to mindfulness of what we are sharing. Our Eucharist is not a real Eucharist if we treat creation as something to satisfy our greed. If we live carelessly, purchasing foods and goods that have involved exploitation of others, then we are offering the fruit of the life of the poor at our Eucharist. We are repeating the actions of the rich Christians in Corinth and those James and Revelation challenge whose meals seem to be more akin to pagan meals.

In the very acts of eating and drinking, disciples are throwing their lot in with Jesus. They make Jesus's story their story by becoming servants and carers to others, empowering creation to be as God intended. Jesus says, "He who eats my flesh and drinks my blood abides in me, and I in him" (John 6:56 RSV).

Echlin challenges us to do something about the debasement of God's creation by truly celebrating God's creation in the very act of the Eucharist. In buying locally grown organic food we can unite the Eucharist community with local family farmers, with local soil fertility, and with wildlife habitats. Such local buying also eliminates earth-damaging long-distance food transport (food miles).[32]

Chapter Summary

Through food we can transform the roots of our culture and lay a solid foundation for cosmic justice. I believe that our study of table fellowship, Jesus's teaching about the Sabbath, feeding the four thousand and five thousand, the Last Supper, Paul, James, and Revelation all clearly support the view that being and making disciples means sharing our food produced, acquired, prepared, and consumed mindfully.

Jesus is calling us to adopt a diet that can transform our world into a place of harmony teeming with life. Thinking of discipleship in terms of table fellowship is parabolic of a community of care whether this is in preparing food and sharing it with others, planting trees, recycling, composting, clearing rivers, putting food out for the birds, or cutting down on our oil consumption. Table fellowship is symbolic of evangelism that brings good news to humanity and all creation, leading them out of captivity and oppression.

Reflection Questions

1. Do you buy fair-trade food? Why or why not?
2. Are the stages of production of foods you are buying considered along with the impact this may have on the environment and populations?
3. Do you try to buy locally produced food?

Chapter 11

PAUL'S ECOLOGICAL TEACHING

Paul is a major voice within the New Testament. His writings are usually at the center of major modern theological debates and controversies relating to women, sex, marriage, politics, and relationships with the state. They have also fortunately received attention relating to ecology.

I devote this chapter to the ecological significance of Paul's work. Of special interest will be Paul's theology relating to Jesus's crucifixion and resurrection. I hope also to unpack the ecological implications of Paul's radical declaration that "Jesus is Lord." We will further consider Pauline texts that speak about the suffering of all creation and the new age on which Paul's hope is focused.

I also examine the ecological significance of Paul's teaching about marriage and sex, which as far as I know has not previously been done. I was initially reluctant to discuss his teaching on sex as I often think that many Christians are obsessed with sex at the cost of other issues. However, in the light of Stanley Hauerwas's and Wendell Berry's works on sex, I am convinced that Paul's teaching about sex should be rooted in the larger landscape of his thinking, especially within politics and creation order.

Crucified Jesus

Paul's good news is the "message of the cross" (1 Corinthians 1:18 NIV), which must be seen in contrast to Caesar's good news of prosperity by military power. Paul preaches nothing but Christ crucified (1 Corinthians 2:2), which is to live in opposition to those human desires that lead to greed and self-interest.

At another level, Gorman observes that "for Paul the cross is not just an act of Jesus Christ; it is a revelation of *God*. In fact, it is the definitive divine self-revelation."[1] The God of Paul is God crucified, which must lead those who are faithful to take up the cross. What does this mean? Jesus teaches that it is better to lose one's life in pursuing justice than to be successful in worldly terms (cf. Matthew 16:25; 23:11–12). The way of the cross is a way of life that stands in total opposition to those values that lead to worldly success. In the first century, the cross was a threat and a punishment that Rome used against those who were opposed to the status quo. Therefore, to take up the cross was to embrace a way of life that critiqued Rome and all that Rome represented; namely, everything that stood for worldly success.

From his early ministry Jesus is on the path that leads to Calvary. In the wilderness he resisted Satan's temptation to gain all the kingdoms of the world and their glory if he worshiped and served Satan. Instead, Jesus embraced the way that leads to the cross. For Paul, like Jesus, the cross was not a garment to take on and take off at will; on the contrary, for Paul it was the life force of his being, driving him to see the world from God's perspective, not seeking profit but looking to the welfare of others.

Practically, Paul's crucified Jesus does not reveal a god who strikes down the Roman Empire with military force. The God revealed in the crucified Jesus uncovers another way of dealing with hate and violence. Paul taught that it is necessary to reject the grammar of enmity (cf. Romans 12:14). This means not thinking in terms of an enemy but of fellow brothers and sisters with whom there is much in common. Jesus's way of the cross seeks to transform the world to the way of God through readiness to die. To do so is both literally and metaphorically to take the road to Calvary.

However, this road to Calvary is not something God wills on his faithful. Rather, the cross is the consequence of human disobedience to God. The cross is the consequence of humans inflicting suffering and death on fellow created brothers and sisters. It is not God who kills Jesus on the cross; it is the world that murders Jesus. Jesus becomes the type of all who become victims of the powerful. Jesus bore the cross because he preached the good news that was bad news to the powerful and wealthy. He suffered because he ate with sinners, healed on the Sabbath, spoke with women, touched the impure, taught the leaders that they were hypocrites, and protested against the Jewish leaders in the Jerusalem temple.

Finally, Paul believed that in living by the cross we live in a way that values the rest of creation. We should recall that the fall of humans led to relational alienation that is particularly evident in the separation of humanity from the rest of creation. To walk the road that leads to the world's crosses is to live in a way that sees all of God's creation as good; indeed, as St. Francis would say, as brothers and sisters. To refuse to take up the cross is to continue living by violence and self-interest.

In sum, Paul's theology of the cross challenges the structures of society that allow injustice and harm to God's creation. Paul's call to action is an invitation to see the world through the lens of the suffering and to give one's whole life to the transformation of those things that cause such suffering. Paul saw that humans are driven to pursue self-interest because of their failure to see how God intends humans to live. The way of the cross is to look not to one's own interests but to those of others.

Risen Christ

Paul could not have entertained the gospel of the cross without the resurrection. Central to Paul is his experience of the living and resurrected Jesus on the road to Damascus. This forced Paul to reappraise his previous rejection of Jesus. The cross without the resurrection would show that Jesus was only a misguided fool, which Paul most certainly did believe before his conversion experience. When he saw the physically risen Jesus, Paul recognized that he was wrong and that the cross was the true way to salvation.

We cannot understand the cross without the resurrection, and Paul would likewise not countenance any discussion about Christianity and ecology without them. It is, therefore, surprising that the early hymn found in Philippians 2:6–11 has not been considered significant for ecology. Echlin rightly calls the hymn "a key biblical text" in terms of ecology and theology.[2]

The hymn in Philippians 2:6–11 summarizes Paul's theology about Jesus revealing that none other than God became vulnerable on earth and absorbed all the suffering of his creation. This is how much God loved what he created. The God of the Beatitudes could not re-create his creation by destroying any of it. The only way is to show the world how its disobedience leads to suffering and pain.

We must remember that Jesus was tempted to become powerful and almighty when in the wilderness, but he refused by walking the way that would lead first to death but ultimately to eternity. Jesus did not take up arms against an enemy; rather, he sought to transform those who were deceived by greed and self-interest, showing mercy and compassion. This for Paul is the basis of life for all who follow Christ. Victory through the cross is hard for humanity because it means not the destruction of the forces of violence and greed, but their transformation. There are generally two ways of relating to an enemy: you fight or you flee. Jesus taught that you face your enemy showing love and mercy.

Therefore, Paul sees God's way of saving Israel and the world as not inflicting violence, but absorbing it.[3] Paul the violent zealot now becomes compassionate (Acts 9:1–19). For Paul, bearing the cross meant to resist the forces of evil that caused violence and destruction in the hope of the bodily resurrection (1 Corinthians 15:20).

The resurrection validates and vindicates the cross. But this is not all: the resurrection empowers believers to embody the cross themselves and validates cruciform existence as the manifestation of the life of God in a community or individual.[4] This way of bearing the cross is radical and political as it contradicts the values of the world, such as hate, violence, greed, and lack of self-control. It means to share and love in a world that keeps and hates. But finally it means to hope that even in bearing the cross the resurrection of all things is on the horizon before us.

Jesus Is Lord

Many would agree that the words "Jesus is Lord" sum up the whole message of the New Testament. Three simple words say so much. However, we have become so familiar with them that we have missed how radical it is to publicly and privately vocalize "Jesus is Lord." In this section I hope to rectify this situation and draw out the ecological implication of saying these words publicly to our world.

No Compromise

Jesus taught that no one can serve two masters, for he will hate one and despise the other (Matthew 6:24). Paul takes this to heart. Paul's life and writings testify to the extent to which he embraced the priority of Christ over all competing claims. He could not serve both Caesar and Jesus as Lord.

To reiterate, the good news for Paul is "Jesus is Lord." This proclamation is a countercultural message. Gorman comments, "This good news was not a private message of personal salvation, though it included salvation of individuals. It was a *political* announcement, or better a *theopolitical* announcement (politics involving God), that challenged—and challenges—the very core of how people relate to one another."[5]

Opposition to Caesar

Paul wrote when the Caesar cult was strong, its battle call "Caesar is Lord." The power of Rome was evident throughout its provinces. Where it thrived there was oppression of any and all who posed a threat to its policies.[6] In declaring "Jesus is Lord," Paul stood implicitly against all that Rome represented, particularly its claim that "Caesar is Lord." Gorman writes:

> If Jesus is Lord, Caesar is not. The imperial claims of peace (the famous *pax Romana*), justice, salvation, and universal rule—through violence, domination, and deterrence-by-crucifixion as needed—could not be true if the one who had freely emptied out his life in obedience to God and love for others is now lord of all.[7]

Embrace, Not Exclusion

It is well known that Rome encouraged elitism whereby the wealthy became richer and the poor became more impoverished.[8] It supported a "peace through oppression" that maintained "peace" by fear through the might of its army.[9] As Swartley argues, Paul's alternative "peace gospel" promised and inaugurated a new order of society, birthing a new socioeconomic, political creation.[10] Swartley writes:

> Paul proclaims a counter-peace, a peace that repudiates domination over others, unites people of diverse backgrounds into the Christ-bond of peace, exhorts believers to welcome one another as brothers and sisters in Christ overcoming hierarchical societal structures . . . and commits his mission to reallocate monetary resources from the wealthier newly founded churches to help the poor in Jerusalem.[11]

Concern for the Poor

The practical out-workings of Paul's faith can be detected in his generous concern for the physical needs of others. His action, for example, of financially supporting the poor in Jerusalem is how he sought to recognize the importance of generosity as an expression of his faith (Acts 11:29–30; Romans 15:26; 1 Corinthians 16:1–4; 2 Corinthians 8:2–4; Galatians 2:10). He tells his Roman readership to give with generosity and be compassionate in cheerfulness (Romans 12:8, 13). He tells them to love one another with mutual affection (Romans 12:10; Galatians 5:14–15).

The appeal for mutual sharing of financial resources in 2 Corinthians 8–9 is rooted in Christ's act of grace toward us.[12] In Romans 15 Paul prays that the offering of the Gentiles may be an acceptable response to receiving God's grace. Paul writes:

> For Macedonia and Achaia have been pleased to share their resources with the poor among the saints at Jerusalem. They were pleased to do this, and indeed they owe it to them; for if the Gentiles have come to share in their spiritual blessings, they ought also to be of service to them in material things. (Romans 15:26–27)

Paul regarded this relief gift to Jerusalem as the crowning achievement of his apostolic calling. Swartley comments, "The peace of the cross expressed itself concretely in mutual care for one another."[13]

The Old Testament teaching about corporate sharing and practical responsibility has not been transcended, spiritualized, or forgotten in any way by Paul. It is the basis, alongside the cross and resurrection, for understanding Paul's actions.[14] For Paul, generosity is proof of givers' obedience to the good news. Concrete economic evidence of fellowship was the essence of a genuine Christian proclamation of the good news of Christ.

Paul is also at one with Old Testament prophets regarding unjust oppressors as he condemns factionalism and sins that harm the fellowship (Ephesians 4:25–26; Philippians 2:1–4; Colossians 3:8–9). Paul teaches that no one repay evil for evil (Romans 12:17), nor are people to avenge themselves (Romans 12:19). Christians are not to be overcome by evil, but to overcome evil with good (Romans 12:21).

Summary

Paul's proclamation that "Jesus is Lord" was not just words but meant living an alternative life that was the opposite of the way of power represented by Rome. Richard Hays puts it well: "There is not one syllable in the Pauline letters that can be cited in support of Christians employing violence."[15] In other words, Paul is committed to cosmic justice, which seeks to transform creation as Jesus did, through love, even to death.

God and Creation

In this next section I will highlight Paul's understanding of Jesus as cocreator with God. All creation was valuable for Paul because his Lord Jesus had participated in its creation.

1 Corinthians 8:5–6 (cf. Romans 11:36)

> Indeed, even though there may be so-called gods in heaven or on earth—as in fact there are many gods and many lords—yet for us there is one God, the Father, from whom are all things and for whom we exist, and one Lord, Jesus Christ, through whom are all things and through whom we exist. (1 Corinthians 8:5–6)

There is only one sovereign Lord, Jesus Christ, from whom and through whom and to whom are all things, Paul writes (Romans 11:36). On coins and inscriptions of the ancient world, the ruling Caesar claimed to be divine and the owner of all creation. Paul, however, preaches another as God and Lord.[16] Paul's claim "Jesus is Lord" puts him at odds with Roman religion, politics, and economics.

In 1 Corinthians 8:5–6 Paul acknowledges the context of pagan polytheism to which Jewish monotheism is polemically opposed and includes the Lord Jesus Christ in the unique divine identity. Jesus is understood as Creator with God of all things. In stating that Jesus is Creator, Paul can be no clearer in expressing his view that Jesus is divine and one in identity with the God of Jewish monotheism. Bauckham emphasizes that Paul's formulation that "through whom are all things and through whom we exist" was a Jewish description precisely of God's unique relationship to all other reality.[17] Paul means that humanity and the rest of creation are from God. God is both the cause and the final goal of creation, both its origin and the one for whom all creation exists. The formulation encompasses not only God's bringing of all things into being, but also his bringing of all things to final fulfillment in himself, in new creation.[18]

Colossians 1:15-20

> He is the image of the invisible God, the firstborn of all creation; for in him all things in heaven and on earth were created, things visible and invisible, whether thrones or dominions or rulers or powers—all things have been created through him and for him. He himself is before all things, and in him all things hold together. He is the head of the body, the church; he is the beginning, the firstborn from the dead, so that he might come to have first place in everything. For in him all the fullness of God was pleased to dwell, and through him God was pleased to reconcile to himself all things, whether on earth or in heaven, by making peace through the blood of his cross. (Colossians 1:15–20)

In Colossians 1, Paul declares that the creative and redemptive work of Christ embraces all things in heaven and on earth.[19] In these verses Paul describes the crucified Jesus as "the image of the invisible God, the firstborn of all creation" (v. 15). The Colossians were awash with images, especially of the emperor. In contrast Paul says that Jesus is God's image, not Caesar; he is the true visible image of the invisible God. The description of Jesus as "firstborn of all creation" does not mean he is the first being to be created; rather, "he is the one by whom the entire creation came into being. As firstborn, Christ is both prior to and supremely over creation."[20] Paul further adds that "in him all things in heaven and on earth were created." By this Paul means "all things have been created through him and for him" (v. 16) and not Caesar. Jesus is also one in whom "all things hold together." Paul claims that creation is held together not because Caesar reigns but because Jesus reigns. Jesus is also Lord of the church. Bouma-Prediger comments:

> Therefore, your allegiance is to your assembly of the Lord Jesus, not the Roman city. Your identity is found in the

church—a community whose foundation story is rooted in the history of Israel and the story of Messiah Jesus—rather than in stories of Roman conquest and rule. Your head is not Caesar but Christ.[21]

In verse 20, Paul says that through Jesus, "God was pleased to reconcile to himself all things, whether on earth or in heaven, by making peace through the blood of his cross." Jesus is the supreme manifestation of God, and his place is beside God as Creator of all things. The importance of the cross is emphasized here. Cosmic reconciliation has been brought about not through violence or conquest. The peace of Jesus is no Roman-style peace. As Bouma-Prediger writes, "This is a different peace—the shalom of the kingdom of God—and a very different peacemaking—one in which a person voluntarily suffers for others and in so doing absorbs evil."[22]

Ernest Lucas sums up the importance of this passage: "This passage brings together creation and redemption because Christ the Redeemer is the same Christ who is the Creator and the Sustainer of the created order."[23]

Neglect of Paul's Teaching about Creation

Douglas Moo rightly expresses concern that much of Paul's teaching about material creation has been emptied of its significance by the influence of Western dualism, inherited from the Greeks. Moo believes this has led to a trend to remove the material world from the sphere of God's ultimate purposes.[24]

I have some doubts about putting all the responsibility on the Greeks. Throughout this book we have seen how human sin is revealed in the extent to which we separate ourselves from the rest of creation. Neglect, abuse, and despoliation of the world damage something that is precious to God, and the cause of this neglect is connected with the fall. The Greeks are simply a prominent tradition that emphasizes the truth of the fall. They have not been the only ones to reject God and live unrestrained lives.

Idolatry

The climax of the fall is the building of the Tower of Babel. Here, humans seek to separate themselves from the very earth/dirt (*'adamah*) from which they take their name and attempt to ascend to heaven. The sin of the builders is arrogance that leads them to go beyond what God intended. Instead of worshiping God in harmony with the rest of creation, humans had become worshipers of the work of their own hands, seeing creation as something to control and manipulate for human self-interest and greed.

Paul particularly challenges idolatry. He sees it as something that leads to the abuse of all of God's creation (Romans 1:25). Idolatry always means rejecting or forgetting that God is Creator. Romans 1:18–23 indicates that Paul believed that human wickedness blinded people to truth, resulting in their making idols as substitutes for the God they do not know.[25] Paul is surely right. Human self-interest and desire blind us from seeing the glory of God's own creation, worshiping only the work of our own hands.

Summary

"God is Creator" is the center of Israel's belief. So it is significant that Paul believes that Jesus shares the divine identity of Creator, an identity that affirms the importance of material creation to God and his overall intentions for his re-creative work.[26] The claims Paul makes for Jesus also have political implications that put the community of believers in a countercultural situation with Rome and its allies. This countercultural message is based on exemplifying Jesus as one who loved and gave himself for others.

Paul and the New Creation

Following broadly Douglas Moo's recent ecological interpretation of Galatians 6:15 and 2 Corinthians 5:17, I too would argue that "new creation" for Paul is the renewal of all creation. In Romans 8:19–23, the cosmic scope of Paul's conception of the new creation emerges quite clearly.

Galatians 6:15

People tend to view the idea of the "new creation" as relating only to humans. Such a view is in line with how humanity thinks dualistically, seeing itself as superior to everything that is not human. Indeed, Paul has a lot to say about the resurrection as a new creation. We must consider what Paul means by this and its relevance for ecology.

"New creation" is everything to Paul (Galatians 6:15): "For neither circumcision nor uncircumcision is anything; but a new creation is everything!" In contrast to the old way of looking at things as expressed in Paul's choice of the words "circumcision" and "uncircumcision," he is setting out a new set of values that should guide his readers. These values are not based on the things of humanity (flesh) but of God. Following these values, there is no Jew/Gentile, slave/free, male/female, circumcised/uncircumcised. Paul writes to the Galatians to refute such dualistic ways of thinking. Paul believes that they get in the way of the new creation. Dualistic thinking prevents humanity dwelling peaceably with each other and with the rest of creation.

"New creation" is a metaphor referring to the entire created world, made "new" in Christ. The background for Paul is the Old Testament and its traditions referring to the total re-creation of the whole universe. Douglas Moo argues on the basis of Romans 8:19–22 and Colossians 1:20 that "new creation" in Galatians 6:15 means "cosmic transformation." He observes that in Romans 8:19–22 Christ's resurrection not only breathes eternity into humanity, but

> the whole created world will be liberated, participating in the glory of God's own children (vv. 19–22). The transformation of the entire universe is part of God's plan for the future, and it is surely the case that "new creation" must include reference to this liberation.[27]

Paul's words to the faithful in Colossae speak also of the completion of all creation: "Through him God was pleased to reconcile to himself all things, whether on earth or in heaven, by making peace through the blood of his cross" (Colossians 1:20).

Douglas Moo argues that this reconciliation, while applied in the context to Christians (Colossians 1:21–23), cannot be limited to human beings. Paul elaborates "all things" in Colossians 1:20 by referring to things "on earth or in heaven." The same idea is expressed in Ephesians 2:15, which speaks of Christ creating "one new humanity," which overcomes the Jew-Gentile divide.[28] Moo also suggests that Paul's "new age" is rooted in the language of shalom, which is found in the Old Testament, especially Isaiah 52:6–10, where all things will be brought into an appropriate relationship to God.[29]

2 Corinthians 5:17

> So if anyone is in Christ, there is a new creation: everything old has passed away; see, everything has become new! (2 Corinthians 6:17)

There is no evidence that when Paul says "all things," he means anything less than Jewish writers normally meant by this phrase: the whole of reality created by God, all things other than God their Creator.[30] The "old has passed away," meaning the old ways of imperialism and greed. As we have seen, one sign of that new creation is the practice of mutual aid in the community embracing both richer and poorer people. In Acts 2:45 and 4:34 property was sold to care for the poor. Swartley writes regarding the significance of generosity and the new age: "The social expression of the new Christ-Spirit reality, a community of love caring for another economically, attests to what Paul declares as a 'new creation: everything old has passed away; see, everything has become new' (2 Corinthians 5:17)."[31]

Romans 8:19–23

Romans 8:19 sums up well the creation of which we speak: "For the creation waits with eager longing for the revealing of the children of God." There is not a day that goes by without something in the news about ecological degradation. Water pollution, deforestation, hunger, loss of biodiversity, and climate warming are just some of the things that we are made aware of and that leave us feeling powerless and despondent.

Given the overwhelming evidence of the Old Testament's hope for the future, particularly in Isaiah, it seems unlikely that Paul, who we know affirms that all creation belongs to God, would think of the redemption of humanity without the rest of creation. Lucas comments, "The general picture conveyed here by Paul is that human disobedience of God means that the natural order cannot achieve its goal, indeed it is falling into disorder. Yet there is hope. The redemption of humans by Christ is the central part of a wider redemptive work, involving the whole created order."[32]

Human disobedience has frustrated the creation's function in relation to God. Christopher Wright comments that the essence of the fall was humanity's arrogant desire for autonomy, rebellion against the authority and benevolence of the Creator. This he observes "affected not only our spiritual relationship with God and our personal and social relationships with one another, but our whole economic and material environment."[33]

In sum, creation has its own voice as it cries out in its travail. God hears this voice, and at the new creation and the "revealing of the children of God," all creation will participate in the "freedom of the glory of children of God." Jonathan Moo remarks, "The implication of Romans 8:19–22 is that it must be fundamentally the same created world that finds its purposes fulfilled and its hopes realized when it is released from its slavery to ruin and brought into the 'freedom of the glory of the children of God.'"[34]

Marriage and Sex

In this section, I will argue that Paul's teaching about the cultivation of good habits regarding sex is akin to developing a disciplined and restrained way of life motivated by love and care of others and the environment. Sex is a fundamental aspect of human life and therefore attitudes toward sex have ecological implications. I argue that to establish cosmic justice we must take seriously Paul's teaching about sex and marriage.

Modern hedonistic attitudes to sex say a lot about our disregard for the human body, which is then reflected in our treatment of other bodies, including the earth. When I refer to modern hedonistic attitudes toward sex, I have in mind the sex that is rooted in hard pornography, violence, as well as permanent and easy access to sex as a form of leisure. The sex I am concerned with in this section is the sex that has become commodified. For many, instead of a God-given gift, sex has become an activity rooted in greed and self-interest.

Today we live as though we were at war with our bodies: feeding them junk, not getting enough exercise, or not allowing enough time to sleep and rest. Such disregard for the physical body of course has its roots in the fall, but more precisely also in Greek and early Gnostic ideas. In these schools of thought we find an emphasis on dualism, whether that is mind/body, man/woman, or humanity/nature. The roots of dualism lie in seeing the body as evil or a very poor imitation of something pure. Extreme forms of asceticism or hedonism often followed this belief, both showing violence to the body through extreme behavior. However, for Paul, sex is a gift like all creation. It is not to be abused; it is to be enjoyed within a permanent and loving relationship.

Yet sex is not a private matter but most certainly a public one. Stanley Hauerwas comments that Christians "have failed to see that any discussion of sex must begin with an understanding of how sexual ethics is rooted in a community's basic political commitments."[35] Wendell Berry also makes similar comments.[36] I am particularly struck by Berry's comments that the disregard we have for our own bodies "is invariably manifested in contempt for other bodies—the bodies of slaves, laborers, women, animals, plants, the earth itself."[37] Berry observes that our way of politics, economics, and sex is based on seeing relationships as "competitive and exploitative rather than collaborative and convivial." Berry concludes, "The world is seen and dealt with, not as an ecological community, but as a stock exchange, the ethics of which are based on the tragically misnamed 'law of the jungle.'"[38]

I am convinced that our unrestrained and uncultivated attitude toward marriage and sex is a microcosm of the human fall, which resulted in relational alienation and abuse. If humans act sexually with no restraint, how can humans act ecologically?

Overview of Paul's Teachings

We know that Paul was single (1 Corinthians 7:7–8). Yet Paul addressed human sexuality in response to particular situations that churches faced in promiscuous societies. The issue of sexual behavior was not peripheral, and he certainly saw it as central in instructing new converts (1 Thessalonians 4:1–8). This is not surprising given the Greco-Roman environment in which he wrote, where various forms of sexual license were common. Paul taught abstinence from sexual immorality, meaning extramarital and unnatural sexual intercourse or relationship (1 Thessalonians 4:3). Paul writes that the faithful should not give in to their sexual passions like Gentiles ignorant of God (1 Thessalonians 4:4–5), but they are to control their bodies. It was chiefly in the disordered sexual vices of the Gentile world that Paul discerned God's judgment on the godless. Many of those to whom Paul wrote had been prostitutes and adulterers and generally promiscuous and unrestrained (1 Corinthians 6:9–11).

Paul is outraged that the Corinthian church is tolerating, rather than disciplining, a member indulging in incest with his father's wife, for such behavior was inconsistent with their new creation in Christ (1 Corinthians 5:6–8). Paul categorized such unrestrained and uncultivated sexual desire alongside greed (Ephesians 5:3).

Paul argued that sexual intercourse ought to be in the context of a committed and loving relationship (1 Corinthians 7). Marriage was necessary and right to avoid sexual misconduct (1 Corinthians 7:2). Sexuality within marriage is to exemplify unity in Christ, where all are equal (1 Corinthians 11:11; cf. Galatians 3:28–29).

Sex, Marriage, and Ecology

Paul's teaching about marriage and sex emphasizes equality and respect for the other. Paul was against unrestrained and uncultivated behavior. Sexual misconduct for Paul, according to Hauerwas, is an overt example of lack of discipline and restraint, which is reflected also in a community's basic political commitment.[39] Paul teaches that the sexual instinct must be cultivated, ordered, and allowed to bring life. He realized that such misconduct was part and parcel of other acts of immorality. Sexual misconduct highlights relational alienation in which individuals think only of themselves.

It is observed by Wendell Berry that promiscuous and undisciplined approaches to sex and marriage are reflected at a broader level both in human community and in the whole creation.[40] A marriage is part of the community, and what happens within the marriage is projected onto the community. Marriage is a kind of microcosmic community, with anticipations in the household of larger dynamics. Sex and marriage create a welcoming household. Greed and unrestrained sex militate against this.

The household is the bridge between the individual and the community, the place where character is cultivated, where work is done both for sustenance and for the formation of care, courage, and simplicity. Within the household, discipline practiced in sexual activity is reflected in central household functions, such as childcare and the selection, preparation, and sharing of food. Hauerwas argues that sexual ethics should not, as it is usually done, be based on the individual. On the contrary, "an ethics of sex must . . . be coordinated with an ethic governing the relations among institutions—familial, economic, ecclesial and political."[41] I would add also "ecological." Hauerwas observes that the issue of sexual ethics and restraint cannot be addressed without tackling the lack of restraint in wider society. Paul's concern with sexual misconduct was rooted in his concern for the wider society with its tendencies to follow its own individual desires while ignoring the sorrow and suffering such selfishness causes the wider community.

Summary

Marriage is a microcosm of the wider ecosystem of which we are all a part. Paul's advice and views about sexual misconduct are strong because such conduct was an obvious and overt expression of the fall. Although Paul does not say it explicitly, misconduct at the sexual level is a microcosm of misconduct at the level between humans and the rest of creation. If sex is simply for gratification, if sex is seen as pursuing self-interest and greed and using the other as an object for this, then we will treat creation in the same way. Our attitude toward sex says a lot about our attitude toward the rest of creation. If we treat sexual partners as objects to satisfy greed, then it is likely that such is transmitted to a wider way of living. Therefore, we must speak of fidelity in marriage in the wider context of developing fidelity to God and his creation. Sex is to be enjoyed within a caring and loving relationship in which bringing joy to the other is primary, and the creation is to be enjoyed in the same way.

Ecological Significance

In this section I bring together the conclusions drawn from my exegesis of Paul and consider how such are relevant to our ministry in facing the ecological crisis.

Whole Creation as the Theater of God's Glory

Paul challenges Christians today to see God's glory in all creation. Our human-centered way of thinking has often led us to see Paul's teaching about God's re-creative work as restricted to humanity. It is necessary to recall that God's re-creating goals are not simply human orientated but for the completion of all creation. Paul teaches that God is not just interested in humans, but in the whole of creation.

All God's creation is suffering and calls out against humanity. The ecological crisis today is a human crisis, one created by ignorance and selfishness, greed and unrestraint. In our human-centered world separated from land and food production, we must work more intimately with the land and make food producers more accountable for the cost the earth is paying for our consumption patterns. Humans must configure new ways and values for caring for, as well as being alongside, the natural world and not at odds with it.

We must look at ways of life that put us in touch with the rest of creation. Riding a bicycle, picking blackberries, going for a slow and mindful walk can help us be like St. Francis, who could appreciate fellow created beings in nature. Paul believed that God was re-creating all creation; if we cannot see the rest of creation as fellow brothers and sisters, then we are far from being redeemed.

The Cross

To take up the cross for today is ecologically significant. It means to challenge a society that acts in ways contrary to God's will. Central to the cross is to look to the interests of others, especially those who are suffering. Each of us must ask what it means to take the road to the cross in this time of ecological crisis. I believe this must involve three words: *care*, *courage*, and *simplicity*.

We must assess our lives in terms of care. Paul in Philippians 2 describes Jesus as one who came to care. Our worldview makes us think of creation as full of commodities and relationships with others in terms of function rather than personal. Therefore, we must look at our lives critically in the light of Paul's advice to the Philippians. I believe, for example, we must examine our livelihoods and the extent to which they water the seeds of self-interest and suffering for others. To walk the way of Jesus, we must make sure our resources are not invested in companies that make profit for only a few people and deprive many others of their chance to live. We shouldn't invest in companies that pollute the environment. We should choose work that helps nourish health for people and the earth.

It is not easy to make wise choices about how we make money and where we invest our money. Yet Paul expected poor churches to support those even poorer. I pray that our Lord Jesus may give us the courage to see the suffering and pain in our world. I pray that Jesus will let us see that someone else's suffering thousands of miles away is our suffering. We must pray to Jesus for the courage to bear our cross through acting to show love and care for God's people and his creation.

The way of the cross also means simplicity, being content with little. Jesus's love of the wilderness was connected with his commitment to simplicity. Jesus spoke of having no place to put his head (Matthew 8:20). Self-absorbed consumption, fueled by willing capitalist markets and their marketing machines, entices us to want what we don't need. We are driven to be successful by making money, owning property, having expensive holidays, even if this means working in ways that are harmful to us and the rest of creation. The way of the cross is to do God's will, living in the present and caring for the future and not solely satisfying personal desires unless those desires be in line with Jesus'.

Sexual Desire

Hauerwas comments that our sexual life is shaped by the fundamental workings of the capital-intensive economy seeking to maintain a high level of consumption for essentially useless products.[42] People's sexual desires are everywhere exploited by books, magazines, television, movies, advertisements, DVDs, and on the Internet. People become victims to this kind of marketing. Christians committed to seeing God's creation as a gift must vow to look after the body and mind. We must ask, "How can we care for the wider environment when we treat ourselves and each other as commodities to satisfy every unrestrained desire?" We can't. Our desire for sex is akin to our unrestrained food cravings; it is not incidental that sex and chocolate are often spoken of in the same sentence.[43] Uncontrolled appetites must be brought under control as we seek to respond to the global ecological crisis.

Practically, we must begin by boycotting pornographic books, magazines, and films, which can lead to the abuse of other humans. We must vow to care and develop an environment that protects others from sexual harm. In working for the protection of women and men from sexual abuse, we train ourselves similarly to care to protect all God's creation. Just as women in magazines are often portrayed as sexual commodities, so also are cars, televisions, holidays, food, and so on. Capitalism is built on commodities, and left unrestrained, it will commodify all creation. Sex is just one obvious example.

Lack of restraint and use of sex for self-interest harm the body as our use of the environment harms the planet. HIV/AIDS and other sexually transmitted diseases have caused untold suffering in our world. Similarly, our misuse of the earth causes great suffering, as does our inability to restrain ourselves from unhealthy consumption habits.

Chapter Summary

Paul understood Christ's work as wider than just the salvation of humans. Paul's hope for the future achieved through Christ's work is cosmic reconciliation. Paul teaches Christians that they are to use their physical bodies in a way that brings glory to God. They are to model their lives on Christ's challenging the values of a world based on greed and self-interest. He called Christians to be generous of their time and resources to support those who were poor. That Christians should treat one another with respect in marriage also suggests that we should treat the rest of creation with similar restraint. In all ways Paul's teaching is rooted in equality and dignity, caring for all, human and nonhuman, as being precious to God.

Reflection Questions

1. How does creation "groan" (Romans 8:22)? What do you see happening today that might be described as the groaning of the earth?
2. Why does it make sense to include the earth in our thoughts about salvation and redemption?
3. Why does the resurrection matter so much, and in what ways does it give impetus for caring actions for the environment?

Chapter 12

JAMES'S ECOLOGICAL TEACHING

James is the most practical of all the writings of the New Testament and the most straightforward in its attack on economic and social injustice. It is, therefore, surprising that James has received little attention in terms of ecological issues. I suspect this is because of the tendency to separate ecological justice from social justice.

A simple overview of the epistle shows a concern for the following:
- The existence of poverty
- The conditions that lead to deprivation
- Those who are oppressed
- Those who literally hunger and thirst for the material items that are denied them by the rich and the ordinary

For James the only blessing and joy the poor and afflicted can have is when they are clothed, given a roof, and fed (James 2:16). We will consider that witnessing against injustice is central for those who are called the firstfruits of creation. In my examination below we will observe that James is concerned with all creation and not only humans. Humans experience the joy of being the firstfruits of creation (1:18) in the following ways:
- Showing mercy

- Being pure of heart
- Establishing cosmic justice
- Pursuing justice as an active form of resistance to those who bring injustice

Those who wish to follow Jesus must embody these characteristics, and in doing so, God's cosmic justice will reign on earth.

The God of James

James depicts God as both Creator and judge, with a purpose for his creation.

God Is Creator

The God of James is the Creator of all things. James calls God "Lord and Father" (3:9). This phrase is more notable by its absence elsewhere in the Bible. In line with this understanding of God as Creator, James refers to God as one who gives rain so that the earth might yield its harvest (5:18), suggesting that God has full control over his creation. James also states that "God is one" (2:19), indicating that God is the only Creator while humans are "created."

James teaches obedience to God and the need to love him (2:5); everything proceeds from this. If James teaches that we must love God, then we must love all creation because it is God's and all good things come from him (1:17; cf. Proverbs 14:31; 17:5). The doctrine of creation lies at the heart of James's theology, and it is inconceivable to imagine loving God without loving and valuing his creation.

God's Purpose

It is clear from my discussion in the above that James believed God has a purpose for his creation. We can investigate this purpose by examining what James states God finds contrary to his will for his creation.

James makes a strong attack on the "world," suggesting that something of God's creation is not pleasing to God. "World" occurs five times in the epistle. James urges humans to stay unstained from the "world" (1:27). The "world" is the place where the poor and afflicted dwell (2:5). God is an enemy of the "world" (4:4), meaning that his peaceable values of generosity and mercy are in opposition to the values of the "world." For James the "world" is not God's creation but the fallen creation caused by human sin. This is what God opposes: idolatry, death, decay, greed, pride, violence, plunder, and inequality. The epistle refers to the "poor in the world," meaning a world that is at odds with God because, in the world he wants, the poor would not exist (2:5). James further describes the world that God opposes as proud (4:6). This "world" that God opposes is to be distinguished from the "earth," which yields its harvest (5:18).

The cosmic nature of God's purpose is indicated in James 1:18: "In fulfillment of his own purpose he gave us birth by the word of truth, so that we would become a kind of first fruits of his creatures." James believes that God has a purpose for all creation and not just humanity as the NRSV might seem to suggest. The Greek used here is *ktisma*, which usually refers to nonhuman creation.[1] It occurs on three other occasions in the New Testament where it refers in the singular to creation as a whole (1 Timothy 4:4; Revelation 5:13), as well as in the plural to nonhuman creatures (Revelation 8:9). For this reason I prefer the NIV translation of the above verse, which ends "of all he created," rather than the NRSV, which concludes "of his creatures," which can be interpreted as referring to only humans.

James 1:18 says that we have "birth by the word of truth." It is likely that the "word of truth" here is the spoken word that God uttered at creation and that expressed and executed his divine will (cf. Genesis 1:3; Psalms 33:6; 107:20; 147:15; Isaiah 55:11). Again, James emphasizes God as the cosmic creator who continues to work with his creation.

What does James mean that our birth was in "fulfilment of his own purpose"? God promises to bring about a transformation in the world so that a kingdom exists where those who love God dwell (2:5b). Humanity is one among many "creatures," and some humans, by their deeds, become the "first fruits" of those creatures (1:18). For James, the firstfruits are the church in its role of living faithfully to God, exemplifying Christ's life, and proclaiming the good news of freedom and healing to all creation.

God intends humanity to love God and, likewise, neighbor (2:8), particularly those who are victims of a society dominated by greed, desire, and violence. James states that God has a strong preference for the poor in the world, those who are the most afflicted of society (2:5) and later described as the naked and the hungry, in short, the homeless (2:15). Elsa Tamez clarifies who James has in mind: "They are poor and oppressed because they have no one to defend them, nor can they defend themselves. They are literally helpless. Everyone takes advantage of them, especially those in power."[2]

James makes it clear that it is impossible to love your neighbor and care for the poor while ignoring the fact that they are hungry and dying from lack of clean water. James attacks a world that daily holds back food from others. To love is to care for all creation so that all are fed. Our status as the firstfruits of creation is not to be understood, as the New Living Translation of 1:18 has it, that "we, out of all creation, became his prized possession." Rather, being firstfruits means that we live in the hope of eternal physical resurrection and live a life seeking to further God's mission to all creation.

James 3:17–4:4 develops what such re-creating actions mean in practice and enables us to understand the goal and purpose toward which God wishes the faithful to work. Peace lies at the heart of these verses.[3] Swartley writes that peacemaking in James

> leads to the harvest of righteousness-justice (3:18) that precludes the envious, arrogant actions described in 4:11–12 and 5:1–6 (also 2:16). Indeed, the two opposing paradigms of life are categorized in James as "friendship with the world," which is "enmity with God" (4:4), versus "friendship with God," which reckons one righteous/just, the fruit of peace (2:23; 3:18).[4]

God as Judge

James also describes God as judge (4:12), meaning that James has a reckoning day in mind. Humans are accountable before God. Those to whom James writes are familiar with an expectation that the Lord would come (5:7), and James says that that day "is near" (5:8). This expectation motivates readers to act faithfully, following James's teaching to love and care for others.

James looks to the time when the rich and the oppressor will be judged according to their wickedness and the poor will have restored what has been taken from them. As God has particular concerns for the poor, the Christian church should be motivated to care and be concerned especially for the poor and afflicted (James 2:1–9; cf. Matthew 24:45–50).

God in Relationship to Creation

I want now to consider what James says about God in relationship to creation and humanity.

Creation's Submission to God

James's epistle is clear in its teaching that all things depend on God. The earth does God's bidding when it yields its fruits, but it can equally hold back its harvest if he so wishes (James 5:17-18). The earth and heaven are both submissive to the will of God, responding to the prayers of the saints (James 5:18). James says that those who doubt God will not receive anything from him (1:5–8). He compares the rich to a flower in the field that disappears when the sun scorches it (1:10).

James is observant of nature and how the beauty of a flower disappears like the wealthy. The important lesson from this verse is that God is above all creation (1:17). Humanity and the rest of creation are distinct from God, and all are to be obedient to him.

God and Humanity

Throughout the Bible, humans act as though they were distinct from the rest of creation and as though they were gods. Human pride causes much pain, and James's teaching attacks this as we see in 4:6: "God opposes the proud, but gives grace to the humble." Donald Carson comments,

> The first responsibility of the creature is to recognize his or her own creatureliness and therefore live in dependence upon, and with worship toward, the Creator and Sovereign of all. The only alternative is the proud independence that is nothing other than utterly destructive idolatry, the arrogance that finally brings down God's displeasure.[5]

Carson's comments are well made, particularly in his observation of idolatry. Although James never uses the word, at the heart of his attack is idolatry in which humanity worships the works of its own hands, denying its own nature as "created." It takes great pride in its own work, forgetting that all things come from God.

James refers to humans as the "first fruits" (1:18), but this does not mean that the "first fruits" are materially distinct from the rest of creation; they are, metaphorically speaking, hewn from the same stuff as all creation. This is why God opposes human pride in James 4:6; central to such pride is the human notion of being distinct from the rest of creation and believing oneself to be the divine creator. This leads to human arrogance and rebellion against God.

The epistle is also a strong attack on the values of the proud revealed in showing partiality to the rich rather than the poor and afflicted. Humans treat other humans as though they are not God's creation, but something substandard. Moreover, James rebukes those who confess Christ yet fail in their duties of care (1:27). The essence of James's attack seems to be against pride, suggesting those who see themselves as being above others, like the builders of the Tower of Babel, set themselves against God and all his creation (4:6–7). In contrast, God welcomes the "humble," through whom creation is blessed (4:6).

James further shows how humans and the rest of creation are of the same stuff when he emphasizes their lowliness:

> Come now, you who say, "Today or tomorrow we will go to such and such a town and spend a year there, doing business and making money." Yet you do not even know what tomorrow will bring. What is your life? For you are a mist that appears for a little while and then vanishes. Instead you ought to say, "If the Lord wishes, we will live and do this or that." As it is, you boast in your arrogance; all such boasting is evil. (James 4:13–16)

This is one of the most ecologically relevant teachings about creation found in the New Testament. Humanity is no more than "a mist that appears for a little while and then vanishes." Similarly James argues, "The rich will disappear like a flower in the field" (1:10). In comparing these verses we find no evidence that humanity can expect more from God than the rest of creation. James draws upon his observations of the natural world and makes a rabbinic-type argument that if the beauty of a flower can disappear, how much more can wealth. James observes that humanity vanishes like anything else in creation. James develops the same theme in chapter 5, observing how riches rot, clothes are eaten by moths, and gold and silver rust. Seeking for security in the works of one's own hands is idolatrous and pointless. Humans are created and are no more or less important to God than the rest of creation. Human pride is sin.

The Likeness of God

In the previous section we saw that humans are created and must take care not to see themselves as being of more value to God than nonhuman creation. However, James also makes the assertion that humanity is made in the likeness of God (3:9), thereby alluding to the Bible's claim in Genesis 1:26–28:

> Then God said, "Let us make humankind in our image, according to our likeness; and let them have dominion

over the fish of the sea, and over the birds of the air, and over the cattle, and over all the wild animals of the earth, and over every creeping thing that creeps upon the earth." So God created humankind in his image, in the image of God he created them; male and female he created them. God blessed them, and God said to them, "Be fruitful and multiply, and fill the earth and subdue it; and have dominion over the fish of the sea and over the birds of the air and over every living thing that moves upon the earth."

Over the course of history, these verses have often been used to justify abusive treatment of humans and the rest of creation. Yet Bauckham has convincingly argued that the history of interpretation of these verses is "strongly influenced by Greek philosophical (mainly Stoic but also Aristotelian) ideas about human uniqueness and superiority over the rest of nature."[6]

In this next section I want to dismiss the possibility that James in any way believes being made in the likeness of God means violently subduing and conquering; I will also consider how James expects humans to act as befitting God's image.

Control and Abuse of Creation

> For every species of beast and bird, of reptile and sea creature, can be tamed and has been tamed by the human species. (James 3:7)

James 3:7 has been used by Christians to argue that Genesis 1:26–28 means the conquering and control of creation. But we need to be careful of such human-centered interpretations of Genesis 1:26–28 and be cautious of being too eager to read James 3:7 out of its context. As we have seen, the Genesis creation narratives don't indicate oppressive reign over creation but more a sense of care and nourishing so as to allow creation to be as God intended.

In my chapter on Mark 1:13, "Jesus 'with the Wild Beasts,'" I argued against an interpretation that Jesus is a wild animal tamer. We find in Mark 1:13 a nonpredatory vision of harmony where Jesus is at one with creation. This is what God intends for all humans. However, an initial reading of James 3:7 suggests humanity is right to tame and control the rest of creation because it is superior to the rest of creation. Indeed, Patrick Hartin suggests that James believes that humanity has carried out this instruction faithfully.[7]

However, humans have by no stretch of the imagination been able to control, for example, crocodiles or many other wild beasts, and I find it implausible that James would think this; it is more likely that James 3:7 is not alluding to Genesis 1:26–28 at all, but rather criticizing humanity for attempting to cruelly control the animal kingdom. Genesis 1:28 has "have dominion over the fish of the sea and over the birds of the air and over every living thing that moves upon the earth." James does not follow the word order, which we might expect if he were following the Genesis passage closely. Also, the word "tame" (Greek: *damazō*) in James 3:7 does not convey the original Hebrew (*k-b-sh*) or Greek translation (*katakurieuō*) of Genesis 1:28. The Greek word used by James indicates brutal forms of domination unlike the Hebrew and Greek of Genesis.

When James says that animals have been "tamed" by humans, he alludes to the idea of the abhorrent treatment of animals for human entertainment. He would be aware of stories about the violent games held in the Roman Amphitheater. In 50 CE, for example, over five thousand animals, including elephants, tigers, leopards, crocodiles, giraffes, lynx, rhinoceros, and ostriches, were killed in one day. Some species of animals were completely destroyed during this period. A rhinoceros would be paired with an elephant, a python with a bear, and a lion with a crocodile. To encourage the animals to fight, they were starved for several days before the contest.[8]

Other uses of the same Greek word James employs here are similarly violent. In Daniel 2:40 the word indicates "shatter." In Mark 5:4 the word appears to describe restraining with shackles and chains as one might use on a dangerous beast. It is not a pleasant word, and there is nothing in James 3:7 to suggest that the epistle is speaking of "taming" animals as a commendable act.

On the contrary, James makes an ironic reference to the fact that while humans can subjugate cruelly their domestic and captive animals, no such brutal "taming" is evident in the control of their tongues (3:8).

Caring for Creation

How does James expect humans made in God's likeness to act? If we wish to understand what it means to be made in the likeness of God, we should consider what God is like according to Scripture. Scripture reveals God as one who cares for all creation and seeks to bring it to completion despite human rebellion. The phrase "being made like God" describes humanity as a whole when it universally seeks together to act like God, who is peaceable, merciful, and just.

To be made in the likeness of God does not mean humanity has the right to use creation for its own pleasures. The existence of human poverty and injustice is an offense to God as is the rape and plunder of his earth. James attacks the values of the world that looks down upon the poor, the mourners, the meek, and the hungry. He calls for communities to live by mercy, purity of heart, peacemaking, and the pursuit of justice, even if it means suffering.

James mentions humanity's being in "the likeness of God" (3:9) in the context of an attack on those who curse fellow brothers and sisters. If one cannot treat another family member with respect, how can one show respect to anyone? According to James, being made in the likeness of God should lead humanity to show mercy as God shows. James portrays God as pure, peaceable, gentle, willing to yield, full of mercy, and without partiality or hypocrisy (3:17). These should form the basis of human action befitting the teaching that humans are made in the likeness of God.

James particularly states that pure religion is to care for orphans and widows in their distress (James 1:27). Here James uses a Jewish tradition of mentioning "orphans and widows" as typical and representative categories of the poor. To be friends of God is to live by being merciful, pure in heart, peacemakers, and seeking justice for the poor, even if it means suffering the same afflictions as the poor in seeking to care for them. There is a choice then to be friends with "the world" or friends with God. The friend of God must be wholeheartedly devoted to God. To be made in the likeness of God is often to be at odds with the world.

I want now to look at the ideas of mercy, purity, peacemakers, and prophets in the context of James.

Mercy. James affirms Jesus's teaching that showing mercy is central and that those who don't show mercy will be shown no mercy (2:13): "For judgment will be without mercy to anyone who has shown no mercy." In contrast, friends of God are to be like God, who gives to all generously and ungrudgingly (5:11): "You have seen the purpose of the Lord, how the Lord is compassionate and merciful." "Mercy" is pure and peaceable (3:17). Those who are merciful receive God's good gifts.

Purity. Jesus teaches that "the pure in heart" are blessed (Matthew 5:8). The pure in heart are those who do God's will by bringing blessings upon the poor and afflicted. The one who is "pure" sees as God sees, which drives the person to work for justice.

James uses a different Greek word for "pure;" but the meaning is basically the same. James describes pure religion as visiting and caring for orphans and widows (1:27 and 3:17). "Purity" in James means single-mindedness to God, while the opposite of "purity" is double-mindedness (4:8; cf. 1:7) in which the impure tend to focus on what is best for them.

Peacemakers. Swartley rightly emphasizes the importance of peace and peacemaking in James.[9] James mocks those who say to the poor and afflicted, "Go in peace," wishing the poor "good luck" or "be happy" while doing nothing about their affliction (2:16). James comments that being peaceable is a characteristic of wisdom from above, alongside being pure, gentle, giving, and full of integrity (3:17). James also alludes to Matthew's beatitude regarding peacemakers:[10] "A harvest of righteousness is sown in peace for those who make peace." (3:18)

For James peacemaking must show itself in practice by bringing good news of prosperity (peace) to the poor, those who lament, the oppressed, and those who cry out for justice in their need.

Swartley observes that James must be read against the context of a "community marked by the arrogance of the rich and humiliation of the poor."[11] He further comments that "the peace" motif provides an alternative vision for community life leading to a "harvest of righteousness-justice" that precludes envious, arrogant actions (James 4:11–12 and 5:16).[12] Swartley observes that "peace" stands in opposition to "wars" and "cravings," where the fruits of injustice are sown in desire and godless longing (James 4:1–2). Swartley sums it up well:

> Justice pursued in peace by those who make peace marks true wisdom and stands in opposition to the cravings and desire that generate envy and lead to fighting (violence), murder, oppression of the poor and wars, and idolatrous pride and slander.[13]

Prophets. James upholds the Old Testament prophets as examples of "suffering" and "patience" while "[speaking] in the name of the Lord," saying that such people are reckoned "blessed" (5:10–11). James uses the same word for "blessed" Matthew uses in his Beatitudes, where Jesus taught that those who are persecuted for his name's sake are blessed, like the prophets who showed steadfastness in tribulation (Matthew 5:10–12; 23:29–36).

James also links opposition with seeking God's will. He calls his readers to live "in" but "at odds with" their dominant cultures. Like the prophets, they are to be ready to suffer oppression and martyrdom in defense of the oppressed and the weak. We are left with a radical and revolutionary image, albeit nonviolent.

It has been argued that, for James, no resistance is called for but only patience.[14] Indeed, patience is held up as a quality of the prophets (James 5:10; cf. 5:7–8), but such patience is not passive. Rather it indicates an attitude of "awaiting," as it were, on alert.[15] Such patience is compared to that of a farmer who does what is necessary in preparing the soil and planting the seed, but nothing can be done to make things happen more quickly (5:7). Tamez writes that it is important that James's readers do not despair but that they continue to sow and cultivate the seedlings, which, for James, means living a life of integrity.[16]

Tamez sums up the importance of the comparison with the prophets when she comments "that James calls the communities to have militant, indomitable patience that awaits opportune moments."[17]

Ecological Significance

We treat this planet as if it were our own playground, sharing it with neither the rest of creation nor even our own fellow human beings. Yet according to James, God has created something beautiful that reveals his very nature as generous, pure, merciful, and peaceable. For James, humanity has mistreated God's creation evidenced in huge disparities existing within human creation and the way humans use land and all creation for self-interest.

We cannot ignore the attacks of James against those who hold back the wages of workers while they themselves grow rich (5:3–4). James calls such actions murder (5:6). We must make it our business today to seek to pay a decent price for the goods we purchase, not leaving people suffering as a result of comfortable consumers who want their goods for next to nothing. James attacks the existence of day laborers whose work is not valued by the rich. What would he say to those of us who choose to be blind to, for example, the wages paid to a coffee grower in Central America or East Africa?

For James a huge issue was the unequal sharing of resources. Today, too, we see increasing numbers of people dying for lack of daily food and clean water. Christians must act toward bringing about food and land reform. In line with James, such reforms should mean giving to the landless and farming communities ownership and control of the land they work. Aboriginal territories must be returned to aboriginal peoples. The land should be entrusted to those who work it and care for it.

To allow unjust distribution and control of land, with the unjust distribution of food that results, is to keep back the goodness of creation from others and to stop them from rejoicing in God's goodness. We are reminded again that the way we eat has an impact on others. As Ruth Valerio comments,

Food also stands at the heart of many of our environmental problems. Consider, for example, the fact that people in the richer countries now eat more beef, pork, poultry, eggs, and dairy products, which in turn means a greater demand for grain to feed animals. More grain means more water is needed for irrigation.[18]

If we are to take James's teachings seriously, I suggest we as a human community think more seriously about land reform with a view to enabling people to have sovereignty over their own land and food. As individuals, we must also make wise decisions in terms of the food we eat and seek to make accountable those who supply us with food. We must act to bring about changes that allow for food and land reforms.

If we don't take seriously James's attack on the rich in 5:1–6, we are condemned by our own inactions. It is necessary to allow people to care in sustainable ways for the land, knowing that the land feeds them; this will lead to the practice of sustainable care of nature resources and conservation of biodiversity.

Chapter Summary

James portrays humanity as a species that is good at dominating others but is unable to control its own actions, lacking in basic self-control. James does not praise the human action of domineering over nonhuman creation in the sense of taming wild animals. Rather, humanity is created by God and is in no significant sense different from the rest of creation. Humanity and its riches will fade away just like the beauty of the flower.

The poor, those who mourn, the oppressed, and those who hunger for justice are not blessed in that their poverty has made them suffer from lack of what God intended for them. In the world there is violence, blaming, quarreling, greed, hatred, and exploitation of others. This is revealed in overconsumption (1:10), even favoritism toward the rich among ordinary Christians (2:1). James particularly attacks ordinary Christians for treating the really destitute and afflicted with contempt.

This is a striking glimpse into how even early Christians in the first century were neglecting the very poor.

Reflection Questions

1. Who were the poor for James, and who are they for us today?
2. Can the wealthy belong to the Christian community?
3. Tamez makes the point that the church acting out of a desire for self-preservation errs too much on the side of worldly conformity—incorporating the society's values and practices. Do you see examples of this now? If so, where?[19]

Chapter 13

REVELATION'S ECOLOGICAL TEACHING

Revelation is the New Testament book containing hideous beasts with horns and teeth; it tells of a coming destruction of many human beings and parts of the earth and sea. Further, and alarmingly in view of the ecological topic of this book, Revelation says that faithful witnesses will strike the earth with plagues, turning water to blood (11:6). Prophets, saints, and apostles will rejoice over the destruction of the city Babylon (18:20). This is not the response of nice people! Christians today in economically developed nations find this contradictory to the nice Jesus of the Gospels.

To make matters worse, Christians who believe that one day they will be taken up into the heavens to meet Jesus as the earth perishes along with sinners often appeal to Revelation for support. Such thinking has inspired, for example, the *Left Behind* novels by Tim LaHaye and Jerry Jenkins, which ultimately promote a dangerously careless attitude toward the earth as simply something that the elect will escape from.

Yet despite these inauspicious details, I believe that the book of Revelation has an ecological message for our planet. I wrote my PhD on Revelation[1] and have published on this book,[2] and I believe it is an environmentally friendly text when it is read with respect to its original literary and social contexts.

Seeing It as God Sees It

Bauckham makes the important observation that "Revelation offers a different way of perceiving the world which leads people to resist and challenge the effects of the dominant ideology."[3] David Smith similarly comments that the visions of Revelation are "life-giving and life-transforming; they lead us from lies and delusions to truth and reality."[4] Revelation is the work of someone who sees God and seeks to show to others what God sees. We can see what is wrong to God and can be motivated to act to put the wrong right.

Revelation is an "apocalypse." *Apocalypse* in Greek means "uncover" or "unmask." Revelation gets it message across by uncovering the truth of our human and earthly predicament. It is an alarming text because it tells us how things truly are, not how we think they are through our rose-colored glasses. Revelation provides visions of how the world is from God's perspective. The Beatitudes tell us that the pure in heart will see God; such words are reassuring, but it is not all good news; indeed it is bad news, for what the pure see through God's eyes is not pleasant. It is a grim and violent vision. If we are to establish justice in our world, we must face the truth of our rebellion against God; Revelation unambiguously does so, but in such a way that is hopeful and provides a vision of a peaceable kingdom of God.

Revelation has proved to be a very inspiring book to many Christians living in oppressed and economically undeveloped nations. This is not surprising when we read that God's promises include food and water (Revelation 22:2) and cosmic justice in a New Jerusalem. Jean-Pierre Ruiz particularly argues for the importance of listening to readings of Revelation from the margins. He writes:

> In the end, both in Latin America and elsewhere, the liberationist optic reads the Apocalypse as a hopeful book, and empowering utopian manifesto that redefines the innocent suffering to which the faithful are subjected as participation in the paradoxical victory of Christ as the slaughtered Lamb.[5]

God and Creation

According to Revelation, God is Creator of heaven, earth and sea and everything that is in them (10:6). God is the one "who made heaven and earth, the sea and the springs of water" (14:7). God is "Lord of earth" (11:4). This last title emphasizes that God is careful and watchful of his creation and that creation is his and that he cares for it. In using the title "Lord of earth," the author of Revelation never forgets that God is a great God with dominion over all the earth. God is not a destroyer but one who gives life because his nature is Creator. This view is emphatically stated in Revelation 11:18, where God is praised for "destroying the destroyers of the earth" (RSV). The idea of destroying the destroyers emphasizes that God is life affirming, rejecting what "destroys."

Creation's Praise of God

Bauckham has been particularly prominent among scholars in observing that in Revelation all creation praises God, arguing that this shows that all creation exists for God's glory, not at all for human use.[6] In Revelation 4, for example, we read of twenty-four elders who sing, "You are worthy, our Lord and God, to receive glory and honor and power, for you created all things, and by your will they existed and were created" (v. 11). In Revelation 4:8, humanity is alongside other creatures before the throne, having the same end; according to Bauckham this end is to assist each other in worship.[7] Together, humans and other creatures praise God: "Holy, Holy, Holy, the Lord God the Almighty, who was and is and is to come."

The four living creatures in Revelation 4 represent the universe's praise of its Creator. Bauckham comments that each living creature resembles one of four categories of earthly creatures: "The living creature like a lion represents the wild land animals, the one like an ox represents domestic land animals, the one like an eagle represents birds, and the one with a face like a human face represents humans."[8]

In sum, Revelation personifies the whole of creation as one raising its voice in praise to its Maker (5:13).

Destroying the Earth

God is passionately concerned for what he has created and works to affirm his creation against those who destroy it. In Revelation, these destroyers are human, and God is praised for "destroying the destroyers of the earth" (11:18). George Caird observes that evil has many forms, "but in the last analysis it has a human face, for it is caused by the rebellion of human wills against the will of God."[9] The value of all creation in the eyes of God is evident where he commands that the grass of the earth or any green growth or any tree must not be harmed (9:4). Faithful humans are also protected (9:4). This would suggest that nature and faithful humanity are at one. Yet humans also destroy.

We learn in Revelation 9 that many humans are devoted to idolatry (vv. 20–21). Christopher Rowland suggests that "the ultimate idolatry is to make the creature the goal and measure of creation."[10] The essence of the idolater is that creation replaces the Creator. To commit idolatry by craving material things is tantamount to denial of the saving power of selfless acts that Christ models. Yet Revelation 9 is in fact an optimistic analysis of the world. It hopes that the idolaters will destroy each other without the destruction of the faithful or the rest of earth.

Earth Distinct from God

The fact that all creation praises God suggests the dependency of creation on its Creator, God (5:13). Although earth is distinct from its Creator, this does not lessen God's care for it. In fact in Revelation the role of God as life giver is developed in contrast to God as a vengeful destroyer. God wishes only to care for his creation in the sense of bringing it to completion when he will be at one with it. God is responsible and has invested his whole being in his creation to the extent that the Bible looks to the time when God dwells fully on earth. Take for example the depiction of God in Revelation 7:15 as one who "will make his *Shekinah* (dwelling) to dwell with them."[11] In this place where God dwells, creation has been brought to consummation, and creation is to worship/serve its Creator (7:15 and 5:13).

Humanity and the Rest of Creation

Nonhuman creation figures more in Revelation than in any other book in the New Testament. Indeed, wicked humanity suffers the consequences of its rejection of God in that the rest of creation appears at odds with it and its evil deeds.[12] In Revelation 12:15–16, for example, we find the earth opening its mouth to swallow a flood unleashed on God's faithful by the Dragon (Rome). Rossing describes this scene as the earth resisting Rome's domination.[13]

Revelation makes no hierarchical distinction between human beings and the rest of creation. Revelation calls humans "inhabitants of the earth," emphasizing the *'adamah* (earth) where humanity dwells (3:10; 6:10; 8:13; 11:10; 13:8; 17:2, 8). As we have seen, Genesis calls humans earthlings or earth creatures (Hebrew: *'adam*) (1:27). The Hebrew word for humanity, *'adam,* is intimately related to the word *'adamah* (ground, earth, soil, dirt). The Bible makes much of this relationship between *'adam* and *'adamah.* The Hebrew underlying the phrase in Revelation probably expresses the intimacy of the relationship between humankind and the richness of the earth.

Revelation's Critique

For many scholars Revelation is the most politically critical of Rome of all New Testament books. Such understanding is helpful in considering Revelation's ecological message for today.

Greed

In Revelation, unrestrained and ungrateful consumption characterizes Roman life. The accumulation of the world's resources in the imperial Roman metropolis was a source of national pride, with Rome claiming divine status by acquiring the wealth and beauty of others.[14] Revelation identifies Rome's chief crimes as violent oppression and economic exploitation. Revelation 18 illustrates this listing the luxurious items Rome plundered from the provinces it had colonized:

> And the merchants of the earth weep and mourn for her, since no one buys their cargo anymore, cargo of gold, silver, jewels and pearls, fine linen, purple, silk and scarlet, all kinds of scented wood, all articles of ivory, all articles of costly wood, bronze, iron, and marble, cinnamon, spice, incense, myrrh, frankincense, wine, olive oil, choice flour and wheat, cattle and sheep, horses and chariots, slaves—and human lives. "The fruit for which your soul longed has gone from you, and all your dainties and your splendor are lost to you, never to be found again!" (Revelation 18:11–14)

Harry Maier writes well, "The detailed listing of merchant cargo (Revelation 18:11–14, 16) describes the way the Earth is mined, slaughtered, logged, spun and sold for the sake of profit."[15] Revelation thus depicts Satan's reign through Roman exploitation as one of destruction, plunder, ecological destruction, plagues, and death.

Destroying the Destroyers

Revelation promises that God will destroy "the cowardly, the faithless, the polluted, the murderers, the fornicators, the sorcerers, the idolaters, and all liars" (21:8; cf. 9:20–21; 22:15). These destroyers, also called "Babylon" and "the beast" are none other than Rome, the metropolis of the mighty world empire.

Walter Wink observes that the Dragon, Satan, who has deceived Rome, also embodies itself in one empire after another.[16] The Dragon is always ready to cast one empire off for another.

Revelation 11

The only way the Dragon can be defeated and destruction end is when communities acknowledge that their sins bring plagues upon earth and reorient their actions toward establishing God's cosmic justice. We will see this is the case in Revelation 11.[17]

In Revelation 11, human witnesses of God appear to cause destruction to earth, water, and other human beings. John states that the two witnesses stand before the Lord of the earth, emphasizing their closeness to God. Those who try to harm them are to be consumed by fire (v. 5). Yet despite being God's representatives, they have authority to bring a drought and to turn water into blood, as well as to strike the earth with every kind of plague (v. 6). It would appear that the inhabitants of earth are right to celebrate when they are destroyed (11:10)! However, as I have argued elsewhere, John is merely remarking here on what the inhabitants of the earth believed to be the case. They were misled by their desire to avoid the truth that the plagues are a consequence of human sin, that is, their own.[18]

The two witnesses are killed by a beast from the bottomless pit (Revelation 11:7), which readers understand to be Rome. The Beast is a force for destruction as its name, Abaddon or Apollyon (Revelation 9:11) indicates. The two words mean destruction.[19] The Beast wants to kill the faithful witnesses because they have uncovered the violence and greed of Rome.

Satan deceives people so they do not see that the plagues and disruption to creation are really Satan's fault. Instead, Satan and Rome blame the plagues on those who proclaim God's Word. Revelation calls Satan "the accuser of our brothers and sisters" (12:10 NLT). Satan deceives the "inhabitants of the earth" into believing that the problem is caused by another. In Revelation 11, the faithful are accused for the plagues, thus allowing the inhabitants of the earth to remain deceived about the truth that the plagues are Satan's—and their—fault. Satan is of course real to John, but this does not mean that John acquits humanity. Satan's reign is embodied in fallen humanity.[20]

In Revelation 11 God's faithful witnesses are blamed for their disturbing words, words that echo those of their Master, Jesus. They are said to have been killed where their Master was crucified (Revelation 11:8). They too are charged for causing social torment as Jesus was (John 11:46–50). Their message does not bring peace but a sword (Matthew 10:34–36; cf. Revelation 13:10).

Yet the torment God's witnesses cause can only be a torment if listeners fail to recognize the truth of their testimony. The witnesses declare that people have disrupted God's intentions for creation. Like the locusts of Revelation 9, people cause destruction by acquisitive desires leading to deception, accusation, blame, and retaliation. Following the moral order of the Beast results in death and decay.

The plagues, rather than being arbitrary destruction of creation by the faithful witnesses, are a sign that God gives humanity up to reap the "natural" consequences of its actions against creation.[21] The plagues represent the consequences of living by deception and accusation, as Satan dictates. Yet in Revelation 11, people cannot see that they have caused their own torment. Instead, they blame those who expose them to the truth.

What hope is there in this situation? The two witnesses are shown to be God's servants when they rise from the dead, a surprising turn of events that leads to the repentance of many (11:13). People are terrified when the witnesses rise from the dead (11:11). Yet many come to see the world from the perspective of the two witnesses and recognize that they themselves are those destroying the earth. Resurrection demonstrates that the witnesses' testimony was correct and leads people to identify the true causes of torment in the world. Their own greed leads to torment. God, far from being a destroyer, intends that people care for each other and the earth, that each may receive life and praise God.

New Jerusalem

The concluding vision of Scripture in Revelation 21–22 looks to a new creation in which God will dwell. This is not just a heavenly reality but the real presence of God on earth, where God's will is done.

In the Old Testament we have seen visions of transformed nature (Isaiah 2:2; 11:6–9; 35:1–10; Jeremiah 31:1–4; Hosea 2:18–23). In these Old Testament texts, as well as in Revelation 21–22, we are given a biblical, and ecological, vision of the future. Christopher Wright warns that such "is not to be regarded as psychological escapism from the problems of the present."[22] Further he writes: "It is rather a vision of what *will* be, because God will do it."[23] Wright asks a very important question that all of us, whatever our theological training, must consider and act upon: "If this is how the story ends, what kind of ethical objectives should shape our behavior as we live in the midst of the story here and now?"²⁴

The last chapters of Revelation, far from rejecting or denying the earth, or envisaging humanity floating off to some other place, looks forward to a new, redeemed creation in which justice will dwell, because God himself will dwell there. John writes:

> Then I saw a new heaven and a new earth; for the first heaven and the first earth had passed away, and the sea was no more. And I saw the holy city, the new Jerusalem, coming down out of heaven from God, prepared as a bride adorned for her husband. (Revelation 21:1–2)

Redeemed creation is what we pray for in the Lord's Prayer: "Your will be done on earth, as it is in heaven" (Matthew 6:10), and Revelation announces that "the kingdom of the world has become the kingdom of our Lord and of his Christ" (Revelation 11:15 NIV; cf. 21:24). There is no vision in the book of Revelation of people being snatched from the earth. Instead, God comes down to earth to dwell.

A careful reader might be perplexed that in Revelation's new creation "the sea was no more." Rossing comments that the backbone of Rome's global omnipotence was maritime trade.²⁵ The disappearance, therefore, of the sea in Revelation 21 is perhaps the most pointed economic contrast between Rome and God's new reality.²⁶ In prophesying an end to the sea, Revelation offers an alternate economic vision where trade in luxury goods will be supplanted by an economy that provides the essentials of life without payment (Revelation 21:6).

Revelation describes the New Jerusalem in inspiring language. Rossing calls the language of these verses profoundly ecological: "The text can inspire us to trust God in the midst of our urban and ecological crises, the crisis of global market economy that marginalizes increasing millions of people, and the crisis of loss of moral will as environmental problems become both more complex and more urgent."²⁷

The New Jerusalem is a welcoming city with no gates (21:25–26) and where there is no temple; instead the entire city is a place of holiness. Those who are outside of the city have chosen to side with the

Beast rather than the Lamb. Those who choose the Lamb and enter the city must leave behind everything that is violent or unjust (Revelation 21:27).

In Revelation 22:1–2, water abounds in the landscape of New Jerusalem:

> Then the angel showed me the river of the water of life, bright as crystal, flowing from the throne of God and of the Lamb through the middle of the street of the city. On either side of the river, is the tree of life with its twelve kinds of fruit, producing its fruit each month; and the leaves of the tree are for the healing of the nations.

In this city there will be no suffering, and everyone will be satisfied. This water is a gift of God (21:6; 22:17). Rossing asks: "Why so much talk of 'without money?'"[28] All creation is God's, and no one has ownership of it. In the new creation, rather than wealth being hoarded by a few rich people, even people without money can have the essentials of life. Rossing adds, "As a healing contrast to the exploitative economy of Babylon, New Jerusalem offers a gift economy in which water and other essentials of life are given 'without cost.'"[29]

There will also be a "tree of life." Again, Rossing comments that "Revelation wants you to share in God's tree of life—to rest in its shade, to eat of its fruit, and to be healed of every wound by its medicinal leaves."[30]

Ecological Significance

I have considered what I believe to be important texts in Revelation for the ecological crisis we are in. In this section I apply this in ways that are relevant for us today.

Hope

Recently I led a summer school on ecology and the Bible. After two days an assistant tutor said to me that members of her smaller group were beginning to feel depressed about the magnitude of the ecological crisis and their own meager attempts to do something about it. As Christians we must of all peoples on earth remain positive because our mission is not our own; it is God's. In Revelation God's victory through Jesus is clearly described, and the saints participate in it (2:7, 11, 17, 26; 3:5, 12, 21; 21:7). The vision of the heavenly city of Jerusalem descending upon the earth must surely be the most positive image we could possibly have of a future of cosmic justice and peace. There can be no excuse for Christians to become negative, proclaiming, "We are doomed!" These final chapters of the Bible must inspire us to remain positive and engaged. We must act ecologically in a positive way.

I believe that the principles underlying the Transition Movement can help us understand the importance of staying positive. Transition US states its mission as follows:

> Transition US is a resource and catalyst for building resilient communities across the United States that are able to withstand severe energy, climate or economic shocks while creating a better quality of life in the process. We will accomplish our mission by inspiring, encouraging, supporting, networking and training individuals and their communities as they consider, adopt, adapt, and implement the Transition approach to community empowerment and change.[31]

Its basic assumptions are listed on its website:
1. "That life with dramatically lower energy consumption is inevitable, and that it's better to plan for it than to be taken by surprise.
2. That our communities currently lack resilience.
3. That we have to act collectively, and we have to act now to build community resilience and prepare for life without fossil fuels.
4. That by unleashing the collective genius of our communities it is possible to design new ways of living that are more nourishing, fulfilling and ecologically sustainable."[32]

The Transition Movement is positive and hopeful in empowering people to acknowledge the gift creation is to humans and celebrate human genius to care for the earth in a way God commands us to. Robert Hopkins, founder of the Transition Movement, contrasts the Transition approach to the ecological crisis to conventional environmentalism. He writes that Transition is based on "hope, optimism and proactive as drivers for action."[33] In being proactive he means taking the initiative in encouraging local action for environmental change.

Transition's own way of working is based on solid psychological insights. Such insights show that the key barriers to engagement in environmental actions are the sense of powerlessness and isolation that overwhelm us and that environmental issues can often generate.[34] I believe that Transition's first principle regarding "positive vision" is in line with Revelation's positive creative vision in chapters 21 and 22. Hopkins writes, "We can only move towards something if we can imagine what it will be like when we get there. The vision we have in our mind when we set out on this work will go a long way towards determining where we will end up.... Creating a clear and enticing vision of our desired outcome is a key principle of the Transition process."[35]

Hopkins would surely appreciate the writer of Revelation with his positive creative vision of hope. In view of Hopkins's words and the imaginative and creative work of Transition, I believe we, as Christians, must draw on the cosmic vision of Revelation 21–22 and adapt its implications to our own towns, cities, and places where we live.

Building and Greening for Survival

On the basis of our reading of Revelation 21–22, we should build welcoming cities where healing and food are plentiful. In order to accomplish this, we must care for the creation and use good building practices so that our cities and our whole planet can be teeming with life.

The presence of the tree of life in Revelation's future city should inspire us to build cities that allow for natural growth, a key element in providing healing and life for all. The God of the city is also a Creator God who, through the natural world, provides us with healing power.[36]

We should encourage local governments to free land for residents to nurture and produce good food. In the UK we have allotments for local gardening that have become very popular in the recent recession but sadly with huge waiting lists. In addition to advocating for increased green space in our cities, we can encourage people to share their gardens and together participate with the land to allow it to do what God intended.

Revelation 21–22 teaches us to look for cosmic renewal and a time when there will be wholeness for individuals, the human community, and the totality of creation. Unless we accept Revelation's invitation to see our own destructive tendencies and the need to begin pursuing cosmic justice, humans will not only destroy creation, but we ourselves will not survive as the ecological plagues of Revelation will become common realities. Fighting for decreasing natural resources, for example, water, will increase. Rivers will indeed be turned to blood.

Earth as Friend of the Righteous

Of all the New Testament writings, only in Revelation do we find the earth working against the destructive consequences of wickedness, as in Revelation 12:15–16, where the earth swallows a flood. Yet the fall has led humanity to separate itself from the earth and soil, which is its friend and from whom its name, *'adam*, is taken. Today we have gone far beyond what our biblical ancestors could have imagined in separating ourselves from the earth. Our urban sprawls are indeed something the builders of Babel would have been proud of. In the UK we find increasingly people concreting over their gardens where once there was wildlife. Land is covered over because people say it is easier to keep the ground tidy with slabs, plastic, and concrete. Some even use plastic grass! Humans want to control and keep nature tidy. It seems humanity won't be happy until it excises "dirt" from its presence. But this has serious ecological consequences.

We hear quite regularly of the damage caused by flooding. Asher Minns of the Environmental Change Institute comments:

> As land becomes increasingly paved and tarmac-covered it loses its ability to absorb rainwater. The rain becomes runoff, flooding rivers, drains, roads, houses and other urban infrastructure. Land development means that more and more of the floodplain surface, because of roads, housing, drains, and packed earth etc, becomes impervious to water. This increases the volume of water runoff and the hazard of flood.[37]

In Revelation 12:15–16 the faithful are rescued from the flood of the Dragon with the earth's assistance. Yet as we build more and more today, we are preventing the earth from helping us by absorbing sudden flooding. We are destroying the delicate balance God built into his creation order. Yet it is not too late to repent and change our attitudes and activities. We can uncover soil on local and international levels, lifting concrete slabs off our gardens, planting trees in our communities, and supporting the preservation of rain forests, so that the earth can be our friend again. This would benefit both us and the earth and truly be an example of cosmic justice.

Chapter Summary

God is Creator of heaven, earth, and sea and everything that is in them (10:6). The whole of this creation raises its voice in praise to its Maker. As a caring Creator, God destroys "the destroyers of the earth" and affirms life.

Human beings are the stuff of the earth, nothing more and nothing less. They are created by God to praise him through their actions of worship and service to him just like all creation. Humanity needs to serve God by caring for his creation and not mistreating it. To do this is to stand apart from all that seeks to destroy it.

Revelation challenges us to witness against the consumerism and greed of today's Babylon and Rome that lead to the destruction of the land, which is God's beloved creation. We must show respect and concern for creation. Revelation calls for environmental preservation, caring for creation as God cares for and nourishes it and us.

Reflection Questions

1. What kinds of human activity might be included in "destroying the earth"?
2. John's vision of the water of life and the tree of life is a clear picture of the interdependence that's built in to creation. The water nourishes the tree; the tree nourishes the nations. How might human beings nourish the earth to keep the cycle going?
3. Revelation teaches us to care for one another and for our world until Jesus returns. What benefits might living in such urgency to share God's love for the world bring us?

Chapter 14

CAREGIVERS OF BODY EARTH

Those who oppress the poor insult their Maker, but those who are kind to the needy honor him.—Proverbs 14:31

I have expressed my enthusiasm for the term "caregiver" to help find a meaningful description for the God of Scriptures. It is a term that appeals to me because of my experience of working as a caregiver and encountering caregivers at their tasks of caring for the physical bodies of vulnerable people.

Many of us in the West have hierarchical worldviews dominated by distinctions between rich and poor, skilled and unskilled, able and disabled, beautiful and ugly, fortunate and unfortunate. But Scripture tells us that God cares for all, and we must be open to an alternative vision in which what God sees as skilled and successful may differ from our own understanding of those terms. Certainly my reading of Scripture reveals a God who sees the earthly landscape very differently from how humans often see it. Indeed, it is God's alternative vision of cosmic completion that motivates him to re-create his world based on visions of nonpredatory harmony.

We must, therefore, strive to understand God's vision for the world so we can work to make it a reality. I believe that the term "caregiver" may open our eyes to a different vision of our mission.

The Bible's Vision

Scripture reveals a God who cares about what he has made and is insulted by those who harm anything he has created. The author of Proverbs 14:31 (cf. 17:5) knew this too well: "Those who oppress the poor insult their Maker, but those who are kind to the needy honor him." This verse reminds us that we should care for God's creation because he made it. Christopher Wright paraphrases it less anthropocentrically: "He who destroys or degrades the earth dirties its reflection of its Maker (because the earth is part of the creation that bears the mark of God's own goodness)."[1] In this section I will reiterate what I have said at different points in this book about the Bible's vision for creation.

The Bible as a Whole

The Bible in three words is the story of creation, fall, and re-creation. The Bible depicts God as one who works to overcome those who harm creation. God works to enable all creation to reflect his glory. It is not accidental that the Bible begins with a green vision rooted in the garden of Eden. It is also significant that the final chapters of the last book of the Bible, Revelation, leave us with the beautiful vision of a tree of life growing beside a river, pure as crystal, that purges human civilization of its brokenness and evil. This striking symmetry between the first two chapters of the Bible with the last two should not be missed.

As Christians we exist and act in the light of the hope of this future where God re-creates the broken beauty of his creation. If we pray, "Your will be done on earth," then we must focus on this beauty and do nothing that is contrary to it. To pray for God's will to be done on earth means that Christians must initiate now what God will later complete, the renewal of his creation, and this is to be done as caregivers treating the earth as carefully as we would touch another's body. Sider beautifully describes this as "the gentle care of a loving gardener, not the callous exploitation of a self-centred lordling."[2] To care in this way is to relate to creation as something having value before God and to relate to it as something that God cares about, as opposed to relating to it as an object that God gave humanity simply to use. Sider's image of a "loving gardener" is a well-chosen one. As a relatively novice gardener I am learning to appreciate this concept alongside that of caregiver.

Caregiving

I want to reflect more on "caregiving" to show how it relates to Scripture. A caregiver is someone many of us are familiar with. Many who read this book will have cared for or are caring for very young children or elderly family and friends. All have been cared for at some point in their lives, and it is likely they will be cared for again. Certainly in Britain when we look in the job sections of local newspapers, we will find ads for "carers," usually with attractive and inspiring headings such as "A job with satisfaction," "Are you tired of your old job?" or "Do you want to make a difference?"

The caregiver, usually she, is someone who doesn't expect to receive much financial profit out of the care she or he gives; caregiving tends to be seen by society as mundane and unskilled. The idea of providing personal care is not valued as shown in the wages carers are paid. This is very surprising as some of us may have entrusted the care of children or disabled or elderly friends and relatives or partners to such a person. How odd it is then that a carer's work is seen as being of lesser value than many other areas of work.

Caregivers are often emotionally connected with the person or persons they care for, and they long to deliver a level of care that enables the persons being cared for to reach their potential as created by God. Despite the poor pay, many caregivers would not swap their work even though many of them suffer from exhaustion, depression, stress, and the hardship of living on less money than most in their society. Yet much of the reward comes from the relationship with the person they care for. Despite the stress, people working in care prefer this work because it is relational in a very personal and intimate way.

It is for these reasons that I believe the metaphorical power of a "caregiver" unpacks the biblical notions attached to the "downstairs/servant"-type imagery of God, which we have explored in this book. Our exploration of the Bible, particularly the New Testament, has shown God as one who cares passionately and emotionally for his whole creation, not as a manager of an estate, but as one who assists another, caring for very basic and personal needs.

I believe that the idea of a caregiver represents many neglected and forgotten skills in our consumer-orientated society. As a caregiver myself I have become more aware of the society around me that values production, power, and success. I have been struck at the extent to which the skills a caregiver has are not valued as skills useful to a consumer society. As a New Testament scholar I believe thinking of God as "caregiver" can help us expose the pro-consumer status quo reading of the New Testament typical of Western Christians and subvert it with a reading that understands God as one who cares for the alienated of our world, human and otherwise.

Property Is Robbery

The misuse of the Bible by today's church consumer society, I believe, is one of the greatest threats that Christianity faces as it seeks to be loyal to the vision of the New Testament. I am concerned at how the Bible's message is often misrepresented, for example, consciously or unconsciously, to advance the prevalent globalizing worldview: "I have a right to it; I have worked for it." Such a misrepresentation of the Bible is like calling a nuclear weapons factory "the Mahatma Gandhi Center."

Those of us in rich nations may not be aware that we are more often the oppressor than oppressed. Bauckham reminds us that the overall biblical story itself took shape mainly in opposition to the globalizing powers of its day.[3] It is not surprising then that the dominant narratives of the great empires from Pharaoh to Rome, whose values were rooted in greed and possession, are severely critiqued throughout the biblical narratives. Unfortunately, this critical and countercultural God of the Bible is easily ignored by many of us who are trying to understand our faith without questioning the privileges we have.

We must remember that God's creation is God's. It is not for sale or something to seize or bargain over; you can't buy it with money or good deeds. In fact, to assume that we own anything is wrong. In a sense, property is robbery. God owns us, and we own nothing and deserve nothing. The idea of possessing property, and the destructive actions that follow along with such an idea, lies at the center of the fall.

God, Humanity, and the Rest of Creation

It has been so easy for modern consumer societies whose inhabitants are separated from nature to forget the wonder of creation and the miracle of food and drink that provides for our needs. Like spoiled children we think we have a right to things and forget that those things are a privilege. Much of the neglect of New Testament study in reference to the ecological crisis has come from assuming that the New Testament does not emphasize God as Creator of a good creation. Such a failure has led to errors in interpreting Jesus's teachings and missing the environmental aspects of them.

Conclusion

God has given humanity the role as his representative "caregivers" to carry out his work. Yet caregiving has wider applications and significance than just caring for other human beings. My new interest in gardening comes out of my work as a caregiver, and that comes out of my training as a New Testament scholar. Caregiving is also relevant to the rest of creation; in Sider's excellent translation of Genesis 2:15 God put people in the garden "to work and take care of it."[4] We must pray that our touch on creation is caring and serving. We have many opportunities to see God's glory, whether that is in washing another's hair or feet or in adding compost to the soil or in eating mindfully. Such "touching" is fundamental to what it means to be a human person.[5]

Four understandings of God as a caregiver may offer guidelines in our study of the New Testament vis-à-vis our relationship with the earth. These understandings are inspired by the insights of nursing care.[6]

- God cares for his creation in that he likes what he has made.
- God has care of his creation in the sense of responsibility.
- God cares about his creation as one who has invested his being into it.
- God cares that his creation comes to have a right relationship with him.

From these it is clear that a caregiver seeks to facilitate life. A caregiver nurtures while recognizing the full potential of the other whether in health or sickness. Caregivers allow the people, plants, animals, etc., they care for to be what each was created for. This vision contrasts with self-interest that treats everything around it as a commodity valued in terms of how useful it is to us.

Caring in our world means putting right the damage humanity has caused to creation as we have ruined so much of the natural world and its life-forms. We have prevented it from being as God created it and hindered its own praise of God. Our touch has been violent and self-seeking, and therefore we do not see God's glory on earth. We have even made God out to be just like us: self-seeking and violent.

The human fall has affected the whole creation and has resulted in humanity being exactly what God didn't want. The failure of humanity to understand its sin results in a society driven by and addicted to violence and exclusion. Our failure to see the world and ourselves as God sees it and us underpins our failure to visualize ourselves as carers for God's creation. Unless we recognize ourselves as but passing shadows before God and repent, we will not be able to care; we will not realize the compassionate, caring nature of God but instead will be destroyers of the earth who will one day ourselves be destroyed (Revelation 11:18).

Reflection Questions

1. Return to the Summary of *The Ecology of the New Testament* in chapter 1. Which aspects of that summary of the New Testament's message do you now understand more? Which aspects do you find particularly helpful and inspiring as you seek to witness in a society that contributes to global destruction?
2. Do you think it is significant that people working in the care sector are often seen as unskilled? What does this tells us about what our world values?
3. Consider how the way we care for those who are personally dear to us informs how we should care for the earth.

NOTES

Chapter 1: Why Care for the Earth?
1. James Jones, *Jesus and the Earth*. London: SPCK, 2003: 5.
2. Ibid., 6.
3. Perry Yoder, *Shalom*. London: Spire, 1987: 21.
4. Ruth Valerio, "Chainsaws, Planes, and Komodo Dragons: Globalisation and the Environment" in R. Tiplady (ed.), *One World or Many? The Impact of Globalisation on Mission*. Pasadena, CA: William Carey Library, 2003: 107.
5. Barbara Rossing, *The Rapture Exposed: The Message of the Hope in the Book of Revelation*. New York: Basic Books, 2004: 7.
6. Mark Bredin, "God the Carer: Revelation and the Environment," *Biblical Theology Bulletin*, 38.2; 2008: 76–86.

Chapter 2: Cosmic Justice
1. http://www.natureofanimals.com/StFrancis.html.
2. Edward Echlin, *Earth Spirituality: Jesus as the Centre*. New Alresford: Arthur James Publishing, 1999: 99.
3. Michael Northcott, *A Moral Climate: The Ethics of Global Warming*. London: DLT, 2007: 164.
4. Job 12:7–9; Psalms 19; 29; 50:6; 65; 104; 148.
5. Christopher Wright, *Old Testament Ethics for the People of God*. Leicester: IVP, 2004: 116–17.
6. Ibid., 117.

7. In *Wendell Berry and the Cultivation of Life: A Reader's Guide* (eds. J. Matthew Bonzo and Michael R. Stevens. Grand Rapid, MI: Brazos Press, 2008): 94.
8. Wendell Berry, *The Way of Ignorance and Other Essays*. Washington, D.C.: Shoemaker & Hoard, 2005: 98.
9. Ibid., 109.
10. Valerio, 2003: 113.
11. Gordon Aeschliman, "Loving the Earth Is Loving the Poor," in NRSV *The Green Bible*. London: HarperCollins, 2008: 91–97.
12. John Lane, *Timeless Simplicity*. Devon, UK: Green Books, 2002: 19.
13. Andrew Wasley, "On the Frontline," *Ecologist*. April 2009: 43.
14. See http://www1.american.edu/ted/chocolate-slave.htm
15. http://business-ethics.com/2010/04/24/1318-which-woods-can-you-use-and-not-harm-forests/
16. Wasley, 2009: 43.
17. http://www.gonzagabulletin.com/2.5539/global-perspective-on-coffee-important-for-consumers-1.853275.
18. See http://www.waterfootprint.org/?page=files/GlobalWaterFootprint.
19. http://www.gonzagabulletin.com/2.5539/global-perspective-on-coffee-important-for-consumers-1.853275.
20. Northcott, 2007: 164.
21. For detailed study of references, see C. Wright, 253–80.
22. Chris Marshall, *The Little Book of Biblical Justice*. Intercourse, PA: Good Books, 2005: 11.
23. Willard Swartley, *Covenant of Peace: The Missing Peace in New Testament Theology and Ethics*. Grand Rapids, MI/Cambridge, UK: Eerdmans, 2006: 28.
24. Robert Murray, "The Relationship of Creatures within the Cosmic Covenant," *Month*, November 1990: 431.
25. Mark Bredin, "Ecological Crisis and Plagues (Revelation 11:16)," *Biblical Theology Bulletin*, 39.1; 2009: 26–38.
26. Hillary Marlow, "Justice for All the Earth: Society, Ecology and the Biblical Prophets" in R. S. White (ed.), *Creation in Crisis*. London: SPCK, 2009: 196.
27. Ibid., 197.
28. C. Wright, 2004: 135.
29. Northcott, 2007: 161; and *The Environment and Christian Ethics*. Cambridge: CUP, 1996: 169–78.

30. Robert Murray, *The Cosmic Covenant: Biblical Themes of Justice, Peace and Integrity of Creation*. London: Sheed & Ward, 1992.
31. André Trocmé, *Jesus and the Nonviolent Revolution*. Maryknoll, New York: Orbis Books, 2003: 22–23.
32. Ibid., 17.
33. Gunther Wittenberg, "The Vision of Land in Jeremiah 32," in N. Habel (ed.), *The Earth Story in the Psalms and the Prophets*. Earth Bible 4. Sheffield: Sheffield Academic Press, 2001: 139.
34. Northcott, 1996: 190.
35. Ibid., 188.
36. Murray, 1992: chapter 3.
37. C. Wright: 2004: 207.

Chapter 3: Ecology and the Wilderness

1. William Loader, "Good News—for the Earth? Reflections on Mark 1:1–15," in N. Habel & V. Balabanski (eds.), *The Earth Story in the New Testament*. Earth Bible 5. Sheffield: Continuum, 2002: 28–43; Seán McDonagh, *Greening the Christian Millennium*. Dublin: Dominican Publications, 2000: 17.
2. Wendell Berry, *Home Economics: Fourteen Essays*. San Francisco: North Point, 1987: 146.
3 Wendell Berry, *The Art of the Commonplace: The Agrarian Essays of Wendell Berry*. Norman Wirzba (ed.), Washington, D.C: Counterpoint, 2002: 99–100.
4. Kenneth Leech, *True Prayer*. London: Sheldon Press, 1980: 176.
5. Ellen Davis, *Scripture, Culture, and Agriculture: An Agrarian Reading of the Bible*. Cambridge: Cambridge University Press, 2009: 69.
6. Terence Fretheim, "The Plagues as Ecological Signs of Historical Disaster." *Journal of Biblical Literature* 110; 1991: 386.
7. Goran Larrson, *Bound for Freedom: A Book of Exodus in Jewish Christian Tradition*. Peabody, MA: Hendrickson, 1999: 60.
8. Walter Brueggemann, *The Word That Redescribes the World: The Bible and Discipleship*. Minneapolis: Fortress Press, 2006: 125.
9. C. Wright, 2004: 300.
10. Norbert Lohfink, *Option for the Poor: The Basic Principle of Liberation Theology in the Light of the Bible*. Berkeley: BIBAL Press, 1987: 37–38.
11. C. Wright, 2004: 157.
12. Warren Carter, *Matthew and the Margins: A Socio-Political and Religious Reading*. JSNTSs.204. Sheffield: Sheffield Academic Press, 2000: 108–9.

13. C. René Padilla, "Globalization, Ecology and Poverty" in R. S. White (ed.), *Creation in Crisis*. London: SPCK, 2009: 181.
14. Walden Bello, *The Food Wars*. London/New York: Verso, 2009: 74–75.
15. Northcott, 1996: 282–94, especially 293–94.
16. Carter, 2000: 108.
17. For further evidence, see Acts 13:6–12; 15:16; 19:19; pseudo-Clement, *Recognitions* 3.47; *Homilies* 2.32; Justin, *Apology 126*; Irenaeus, *Contra Haereses* 1.23; Lucian, *Alexander 24–33*; *De Syria* 10; Eusebius, *H.E.* 2.13–14; Theophilus, *Ad Autolycum* 1.8. See also discussion in Gregory K. Beale, *The Book of Revelation*. NIGTC. Grand Rapids, MI: Eerdmans, 1999: 711.
18. Carter, 2000: 110.

Chapter 4: Jesus "with the Wild Beasts" (Mark 1:13)
1. Thomas Berry, *The Great Work: Our Way into the Future*. New York: Three Rivers Press, 1999: 48.
2. Yann Arthus-Bertrand, *A Hymn to the Planet and Humanity*. New York: Abrams, 2005: 8.
3. http://www.charitywater.org/whywater/.
4. Yann Arthus-Bertrand, 2005: 22.
5. Murray, 1992: 99.
6. C. Wright, 2004: 121.
7. Richard Bauckham "Jesus and the Wild Animals (Mark 1:13): A Christological Image for an Ecological Age," in J. Green and M. Turner (eds.), *Jesus of Nazareth Lord and Christ: Essays on the Historical Jesus and New Testament Christology*. Grand Rapids, MI: Eerdmans, 1994: 10.
8. Bauckham, 1994: 15–16.
9. Report to World Council of Churches, *The Liberation of Life*, reprinted in Charles Birch, William Eakin, Jay B. MacDaniel (eds.), *Liberating Life: Contemporary Approaches to Ecological Theology*. Maryknoll, NY: Orbis Books, 1990: see appendix.
10. "Jesus and Animals II: What Did He Practise?" in A. Linzey and D. Yamamoto (eds.), *Animals on the Agenda*. London: SCM, 1998: 59.

Chapter 5: Bad News
1. Edward Echlin, *The Cosmic Circle: Jesus & Ecology*. Dublin: The Columba Press, 2004: 67.

2 John Nolland, *Luke 1.–9:20*. Word Biblical Commentary 35a. Dallas, TX: Word Books, 1989: 283.
3. Jones, 2003: 90.
4. Nolland, 1989: 197.
5. C. Wright, 2004: 179.
6. John Kavanaugh, *Following Christ in a Consumer Society*. Maryknoll, New York: Orbis Books, 1981: 90; affirms poverty so that we can be freed from the oppression and enslavement of wealth.
7. Richard Bauckham, *James*. New Testament Reading. London: Routledge, 1999: 188.
8. Joachim Jeremias, *Jesus's Promise to the Nations*. Studies in Biblical Theology 24. Naperville, IL: Alec R. Allenson, 1958: 45.
9. *The Isaiah Targum, The Aramaic Bible II,* trans. Bruce D. Chilton. Edinburgh: T&T Clark, 1987: 118–19.
10. Kenneth Bailey, *Jesus through Middle Eastern Eyes*. London: SPCK, 2008: 298.
11. Ibid., 304.
12. N. T. Wright, *Jesus and the Victory of God*. London: SPCK, 1996: 536; Echlin, 2004: 65.
13. Bauckham, "Jesus, God and Nature in the Gospels," in R. S. White (ed.), *Creation in Crisis*. London: SPCK, 2009: 211.
14. Echlin, 2004: 99.
15. Bauckham, 2009: 217.
16. C. Wright, 2004: 186.
17. Robert White, "Natural Disasters: Acts of God or Results of Human Folly?" in R. S. White (ed.), *Creation in Crisis*. London: SPCK, 2009: 119.
18. Seán McDonagh, *To Care for the Earth*. London: Geoffrey Chapman, 1986: 35.
19. Wangari Maathai, *Unbowed: One Woman's Story*. London: Arrow Press, 2008: 121.
20. Ibid., 123.
21. Piers Blaikie, *The Political Economy of Soil Erosion in Developing Countries*. London: Longman, 1985: 58–59; Northcott, 1996: 15.
22. Amartyr Sen, *Development as Freedom*. Oxford: OUP, 1999: 162–80.
23. Teresa Hayter, *The Creation of World Poverty: An Alternative View to Brandt Report*. London: Pluto Press, 1982: 31–32.

24. Wayne Roberts, *The No-Nonsense Guide to World Food*. Oxford: New Internationalist, 2008.
25. Richard Horsley, *Jesus and the Spiral of Violence*. Minneapolis: Fortress Press, 1993: 251.
26. Mark 10:17–30; Matthew 6:2–4; 7:7–11; Luke 6:35, 38; 8:1–3; 12:32–34; 14:25–35;19:1–10, John 12:6; 13:29.
27. Matthew 6:19–34; Luke 12:22–31.
28. Mark 6:7–13; cf. Luke 9:3; 10:4.
29. Mark 4:19 NASB.

Chapter 6: The Beatitudes 1: Matthew 5:3–6

1. Frederick Bruner, *The Christbook: Matthew 1–12*. Grand Rapids, MI: Eerdmans, 2004: 157.
2. Carter, 2000: 131.
3. The Aramaic Targum paraphrases "Your God reigns" with "the kingdom of your God is revealed."
4. When Jesus says "For you always have the poor with you" he does not passively acquiesce to poverty in society (Matthew 26:11). Jesus's words are an implied criticism as, according to Deuteronomy 15:11, enduring poverty was evidence of Israel's failure to keep the laws of the covenant, which would have removed poverty. C. Marshall, 2005: 54.
5. Artur Weiser, *The Psalms*. Old Testament Library. London: SCM, 1962: 312.
6. William D. Davies and Dale C. Allison, *Matthew 1–7*. ICC. Volume 1. London: T&T Clark, 1988: 449.
7. Carter, 2000: 133.
8. Glen Stassen, *Living the Sermon on the Mount*. San Francisco, CA: Jossey-Bass, 2006: 39.
9. Carter, 2000: 134.
10. Maathai, 2008: 121–22.

Chapter 7: The Beatitudes 2: Matthew 5:7–12

1. http:www.dropthedebt.org.
2. Maathai, 2008: 277.
3. Maathai, 2008: 280.
4. http:www.dropthedebt.org/.
5. Peter Selby, *Grace and Mortgage*. London: DLT, 1997: 86. For further research see James Kahn and Judith McDonald, "Third World Debt and Tropical

Deforestation," *Ecological Economics* 12.1; February 1995: 107–23. See also http://www.esd.ornl.gov/iab/iab3-11.htm.

6. Christopher Rowland, "Apocalyptic, the Poor, and the Gospel of Matthew," *JTS* 45, 1994: 509.

7. David Strahan retrieved from http://news.bbc.co.uk/1/hi/sci/tech/6505127.stm. For further discussion see Robert Hopkins, *The Transition Handbook*. Devon, UK: Green Books, 2008: 21.

8. Cited in Robert Hopkins, 2008: 23.

9. John Vidal in *Observer* article on http://www.guardian.co.uk/world/2010/may/30/oil-spills-nigeria-niger-delta-shell.

10. Carter, 2000: 270.

11. Ibid.

12. See Bruce D. Chilton, trans., *The Isaiah Targum, The Aramaic Bible II*. Edinburgh: T&T Clark, 1987

13. Valerio, 2003: 110.

14. http://globalpolicy.org/the-dark-side-of-natural-resources/water-in-conflict.html.

15. Valerio, 2003: 111.

16. Ibid., 43.

17. Ibid.

18. Bruner, 2004: 181–82.

19. Ibid., 182.

Chapter 8: The Lord's Prayer 1: Matthew 6:9–10

1. Carter, 2000: 163.

2. Ibid., 161.

3. Ibid., 163–64.

4. Jonathan Pennington, *Heaven and Earth in the Gospel of Matthew*. Grand Rapids, MI: Baker Academic, 2007: 86.

5. Sean Freyne, *Jesus, a Jewish Galilean: A New Reading of the Jesus-Story*. London: T&T Clark, 2004: 38.

6. Bailey, 2008: 99.

7. Echlin, 1999: 121.

8. Translation from Brother Ramon, *Franciscan Spirituality*. London: SPCK, 1994: 139.

9. Ibid., 130.

10. Ibid.

11. Echlin, 1999: 127.
12. Ibid., 129–30.
13. Pennington, 2007: 155.
14. Ibid.,133–34.
15. Bruner, 2004: 297.
16. Bauckham, "Joining Creation's Praise of God," *Ecotheology* 7.1; 2002b: 47.
17. Bruner, 2004: 99.
18. Bauckham, 2009: 212.
19. Swartley, 2006: 15–19.
20. Wendell Berry, *Jayber Crow*. Washington, D.C.: Counterpoint, 2000: 220.
21. Jürgen Moltmann, *God in Creation*. London: SCM, 1985: 162.
22. Ibid., 182.
23. Ibid., 183–84.
24. Ibid., 181.
25. Bailey, 2008: 118. Italics are in original.

Chapter 9: The Lord's Prayer 2: Matthew 6:11-13

1. Italics are in original.
2. Bailey, 2008: 123.
3. Carter, 2000: 166.
4. Ibid., 167.
5. W. Berry quoted by John Lane, 2002: 91.
6. Sharon Ringe, *Jesus, Liberation, and the Biblical Jubilee*. Eugene: Wipf&Stock, 1985: 83.
7. Ibid., 77.
8. Echlin, 1999: 98.
9. Carter, 2000: 345.
10. Stassen, 2006: 122.
11. Ringe, 1985: 77.

Chapter 10: Food Makes the World Go Round

1. Carolyn Steel, "City, Sitopia," *Ecologist*, June 2009: 19.
2. Marcus Borg, *Jesus: A New Vision*. New York: Harper, 1987: 133.
3. Pliny the Younger, *Letter* 2.6; cf. Luke 14:7.
4. Timothy Gorringe, *The Sign of Love: Reflections on the Eucharist*. London: SPCK, 1997: 19.
5. Ibid., 20.

6. Petronius, *Satyricon* 44.
7. Carter, 2000: 263.
8. Ibid., 265.
9. Ibid., 266.
10. Richard France, *Matthew*. Tyndale New Testament Commentaries. Leicester: IVP, 1985: 248–49; also Ched Myers, *Binding the Strong Man*. Maryknoll: New York: Orbis; 2002: 206–10.
11. Carter, 2000: 305.
12. Gorringe, 1997: 34.
13. Echlin, 1999: 97.
14. Davies and Allison, 1988: 470.
15. Echlin, 1999: 97.
16. Gorringe, 1997: 52.
17. William Davies and Dale Allison, *Matthew 19–28*. ICC. Volume 3. London: T&T Clark, 1997: 470.
18. Carter, 2000: 507.
19. Northcott, 2007: 254.
20. Ibid., 252.
21. Ibid.
22. Ibid.
23. Ibid., 254.
24. Richard Bauckham, *The Theology of the Book of Revelation*. Cambridge: CUP, 1993: 34–40.
25. J. Nelson Kraybill, *Imperial Cult and Commerce in John's Apocalypse*. JSNTS 132. Sheffield: Sheffield Academic Press, 1996.
26. Seneca, *Epistulae Morales* 10.2
27. Bauckham, 1993: 124.
28. Richard Bauckham, *The Theology of Jürgen Moltmann*. Edinburgh: T&T Clark, 1995: 39.
29. William Tuttle, "What Then Should We Eat?" *Resurgence* 252; 2008: 38.
30. John Lane, 2002: 22.
31. Leech, 1980: 110.
32. Echlin, 1999: 98.

Chapter 11: Paul's Ecological Teaching
1. Michael Gorman, *Reading Paul*. Milton Keynes: Paternoster, 2008: 79.
2. Echlin, *Climate and Christ*. Dublin: Columba, 2010: 43.

3. Gorman, 2008: 95.
4. Ibid., 147.
5. Ibid., 41.
6. Swartley, 2006: 247.
7. Gorman, 2008: 102.
8. Kraybill, 1996: 22.
9. Michael Gorman, *Cruciformity: Paul's Narrative Spirituality of the Cross*. Grand Rapids: Eerdmans, 2001: 270.
10. Swartley, 2006: 251.
11. Ibid., 250.
12. Ibid., 219.
13. Ibid., 221.
14. C. Wright, 2004: 193.
15. Richard Hays, *The Moral Vision of the New Testament: A Contemporary Introduction to New Testament Ethics*. London: Continuum T&T Clark, 1997: 331.
16. Swartley, 2006: 237.
17. Bauckham, 2009: 215.
18. Ibid., 216.
19. Elma Flor, "The Cosmic Christ and Ecojustice in the New Cosmos (Ephesians 1)," in N. Habel & V. Balabanski (eds.), *The Earth Story in the New Testament*. Earth Bible 5. Sheffield: Continuum, 2002: 141.
20. Steven Bouma-Prediger, *For the Beauty of the Earth: A Christian Vision for Creation Care*. Grand Rapids, MI: Baker Academic, 2001: 106.
21. Ibid., 107.
22. Ibid., 108.
23 Ernest Lucas, "The New Testament Teaching on the Environment," *Transformation* 16:3; 1999: 96–97.
24. Douglas Moo, "Creation and New Creation," in R. S. White (ed.), *Creation in Crisis*. London: SPCK, 2009: 51.
25. Swartley, 2006: 225.
26. Gorman, 2008: 104.
27. D. Moo, 2009: 247.
28. Lucas, 1999: 96.
29. D. Moo, 2009: 248.
30. Bauckham, 2009: 216.
31. Swartley, 2006: 174.

32. Lucas, 1999: 96.
33. C. Wright, 2004: 250.
34. Jonathan Moo, "Environmental Unsustainability and a Biblical Vision of the Earth's Future," in R. S. White (ed.), *Creation in Crisis*. London: SPCK, 2009: 260.
35. Stanley Hauerwas, "Sex in Public: How Adventurous Christians Are Doing It," in J. Berkman and M. Cartrwright (eds.), *The Hauerwas Reader*. Durham and London: Duke University Press, 2001: 489.
36. Wendell Berry, *Sex, Economy, Freedom & Community*. New York: Pantheon, 1993.
37. W. Berry, 2002: 101.
38. Ibid.
39. Hauerwas, 2001: 489.
40. W. Berry, 1993: 166–67
41. Hauerwas, 2001: 494.
42. Ibid., 495–96.
43. See for example: http://www.chocolate.org/misc/hot-chocolate.html.

Chapter 12: James's Ecological Teaching
1. Sophie Laws, *A Commentary on the Epistle of James*. Black New Testament Commentaries. London: Adam & Charles Black, 1980: 78.
2. Elsa Tamez, *The Scandalous Message of James*. New York: A Crossroad Book, 2002: 17.
3. Swartley, 2006: 261.
4. Ibid.
5. Donald A. Carson, "James" in G. K. Beale and D. A. Carson (eds.), *Commentary on the New Testament Use of the Old Testament*. Grand Rapids, MI: Baker Academic, 2007: 1009.
6. Richard Bauckham, *God and the Crisis of Freedom*. Louisville/London: Westminster John Knox Press, 2002a: 132.
7. Patrick J Hartin, *James*. Sacra Pagina 14. Collegeville, Minnesota: Liturgical Press, 2003: 186.
8. http://www.spartacus.schoolnet.co.uk/ROMgames.htm.
9. Swartley, 2006: 259–62.
10. Laws, 1980: 165; Martin, 1988: 138; Tamez, 2002: 73.
11. Swartley, 2006: 260.
12. Ibid., 261.

13. Ibid., 262.
14. Peter Davids, *Commentary on James*. NIGNTC. Grand Rapids, MI: Eerdmans, 1982: 171.
15. Tamez, 2002: 45.
16. Ibid.
17. Ibid., 46.
18. Valerio, 2003: 117.
19. Questions from Pamela Sparr in Tamez, 2003: 105.

Chapter 13: Revelation's Ecological Teaching

1. Mark Bredin. *Jesus, Revolutionary of Peace: A Nonviolent Christology in the Book of Revelation*. PBM. Carlisle: Paternoster, 2003.
2. Mark Bredin, "God the Carer: Revelation and the Environment," *Biblical Theology Bulletin*, 38.2. 2008: 76-86
3. Bauckham, 1993: 159.
4. David Smith, *Against the Stream: Christianity and Mission in an Age of Globalization*. Leicester, UK: IVP, 2003: 42.
5. Jean-Pierre Ruiz, "Taking a Stand in the Sand on the Seashore: A Postcolonial Exploration of Revelation 13," in David L. Barr (ed.), *Reading the Book of Revelation*. Atlanta, GA: SBL, 2003: 122.
6. Bauckham, "Creation's Praise of God in the Book of Revelation," *Biblical Theology Bulletin* 38.2; 2008: 55.
7. Bauckham, 2002a: 177.
8. Bauckham, 2008: 60.
9. George Caird, *The Revelation of St. John the Divine*. Black's New Testament Commentaries. 2nd ed. London: A&C Black, 1984: 120.
10. Christopher Rowland, *Revelation*. Epworth Commentaries. London: Epworth Press, 1993: 95.
11. Leon Morris, *Revelation*. Tyndale New Testament Commentaries. Leicester: IVP, 1969: 118.
12. John Sweet, *Revelation*. London: SCM, 1990: 165.
13. Barbara Rossing , "River of Life in God's New Jerusalem: An Eschatological Vision for Earth's Future," in *Christianity and Ecology*, R. R. Ruether and D. Hessel (eds.). Cambridge, MA: Harvard University Press; Center for World Religions, 1999: 189.
14. Richard Horsley, *Jesus and Empire: The Kingdom of God and the New World Disorder*. Minneapolis: Fortress Press, 2003: 30.

15. Harry Maier, "There Is a New World Coming! Reading the Apocalypse in the Shadow of the Canadian Rockies," in N. Habel & V. Balabanski (eds.), *The Earth Story in the New Testament*. Earth Bible 5. Sheffield: Continuum, 2002: 176.
16. Walter Wink, *Engaging the Powers*. Minneapolis: Fortress Press, 1992: 91.
17. A fuller treatment of this text can be found in Mark Bredin, "Ecological Crisis and Plagues (Revelation 11:16)," *Biblical Theology Bulletin*, 39.1; 2009: 26–38.
18. Bredin, 2009: 27–28 and 30–31.
19. John Sweet, *Revelation*. London: SCM, 1990: 170.
20. See René Girard, *I See Satan Fall like Lightning*. Maryknoll: New York, 2001.
21. Fretheim, 1991: 386; Bredin 2009: 28.
22. C. Wright, 2004: 186.
23. Ibid.
24. Ibid.
25. Rossing, 1999: 207.
26. Ibid., 212–13.
27. Ibid., 214.
28. Rossing, 2004: 153.
29. Ibid.
30. Ibid., 154.
31. http://www.transitionus.org/about-us.
32. Ibid.
33. Robert Hopkins, *The Transition Handbook: From Oil Dependency to Local Resilience*. Devon, UK: Green Books, 2008: 135.
34. Ibid., 142.
35. Ibid., 141.
36. Rossing, 2004: 155–56.
37. http://climatex.org/articles/climate-change-info/flooding-introduction/.

Chapter 14: Caregivers of Body Earth
1. C. Wright, 2004: 106–7.
2. Ronald J. Sider, "Biblical Foundations for Creation Care," in R. J. Berry (ed.), *The Care of Creation*. Leicester, UK: IVP, 2000: 48.
3. Richard Bauckham, *Bible and Mission: Christian Witness in a Postmodern World*. Bletchley: Paternoster, 2003: 103.

4. Sider, 2000: 47–48.
5. John Swinton and Esther Mcintosh, "Persons in Relation: The Care of Persons with Learning Disabilities," *Theology Today* 157; 2001: 179.
6. Cf. Jeffrey Blustein, *Care and Commitment*. New York/London: OUP, 1991: 28.

BIBLIOGRAPHY

Aeschliman, Gordon "Loving the Earth Is Loving the Poor," in NRSV *The Green Bible*. London: HarperCollins, 2008: 91–97.

Arthus-Bertrand Yann, *A Hymn to the Planet and Humanity*. New York: Abrams, 2005.

Bailey, Kenneth, *Jesus through Middle Eastern Eyes*. London: SPCK, 2008.

Bauckham, Richard, *The Theology of the Book of Revelation*. Cambridge: Cambridge University Press, 1993.

———, "Jesus and the Wild Animals (Mark 1:13): A Christological Image for an Ecological Age," in J. Green and M. Turner (eds.), *Jesus of Nazareth Lord and Christ: Essays on the Historical Jesus and New Testament Christology*. Grand Rapids, MI: Eerdmans, 1994: 3–21.

———, *The Theology of Jürgen Moltmann*. Edinburgh: T&T Clark, 1995.

———, "Jesus and Animals I: What Did He Teach?" in A. Linzey and D. Yamamoto (eds.), *Animals on the Agenda*. London: SCM, 1998: 33–48.

———, "Jesus and Animals II: What Did He Practise?" in A. Linzey and D. Yamamoto (eds.), *Animals on the Agenda*. London: SCM, 1998: 49–60.

———, *James*. New Testament Reading. London: Routledge, 1999.

———, *God and the Crisis of Freedom*. Louisville/London: Westminster John Knox Press, 2002a.

———, "Joining Creation's Praise of God," *Ecotheology* 7.1; 2002b: 45–49.

———, *Bible and Mission: Christian Witness in a Postmodern World*. Bletchley: Paternoster, 2003.

———, "Creation's Praise of God in the Book of Revelation," *Biblical Theology Bulletin* 38.2; 2008: 55–63.

———, "Jesus, God and Nature in the Gospels," in R. S. White (ed.), *Creation in Crisis*. London: SPCK, 2009: 209–24.

Bello, Walden, *The Food Wars*. London/New York: Verso, 2009.

Berry, Thomas, *The Great Work: Our Way into the Future*. New York: Three Rivers Press, 1999.

Berry, Wendell, *Home Economics: Fourteen Essays*. San Francisco: North Point, 1987.

———, *Sex, Economy, Freedom & Community*. New York: Pantheon, 1993.

———, *Jayber Crow*. Washington, D.C.: Counterpoint, 2000.

———, *The Art of the Commonplace: The Agrarian Essays of Wendell Berry*. Norman Wirzba (ed.), Washington, D.C: Counterpoint, 2002.

———, *The Way of Ignorance and Other Essays*. Washington, D.C.: Shoemaker & Hoard, 2005.

Blaikie, Piers, *The Political Economy of Soil Erosion in Developing Countries*. London: Longman, 1985.

Blustein, Jeffrey, *Care and Commitment*. New York/London: OUP, 1991.

Bonzo, J. Matthew, and Michael R. Stevens, *Wendell Berry and the Cultivation of Life: A Reader's Guide*. Grand Rapids, MI: Brazos Press, 2008.

Borg, Marcus, *Conflict, Holiness & Politics in the Teachings of Jesus*. Studies in the Bible and Early Christianity 5. New York: Mellen Press, 1984.

———, *Jesus: A New Vision*. New York: Harper, 1987.

Bouma-Prediger, Steven, *For the Beauty of the Earth: A Christian Vision for Creation Care*. Grand Rapids, MI: Baker Academic, 2001.

Bredin, Mark, *Jesus, Revolutionary of Peace: A Nonviolent Christology in the Book of Revelation*. PBM. Carlisle: Paternoster, 2003.

———, "God the Carer: Revelation and the Environment," *Biblical Theology Bulletin*, 38.2. 2008: 76–86.

———, "Ecological Crisis and Plagues (Revelation 11:16)," *Biblical Theology Bulletin*, 39.1. 2009: 26–38.

Brueggemann, Walter, *The Word That Redescribes the World: The Bible and Discipleship*. Minneapolis: Fortress Press, 2006.

Bruner, Frederick D., *The Christbook: Matthew 1–12*. Grand Rapids, MI: Eerdmans, 2004.

Caird, George B. *The Revelation of St. John the Divine*. 2nd ed. Black's New Testament Commentaries. London: A&C Black, 1984.

Carson, Donald A., "James" in G. K. Beale and D. A. Carson (eds.), *Commentary on the New Testament Use of the Old Testament*. Grand Rapids, MI: Baker Academic, 2007: 997–1013.

Carter, Warren, *Matthew and the Margins: A Socio-Political and Religious Reading*. JSNTSs. 204. Sheffield: Sheffield Academic Press, 2000.

Chilton, Bruce D., trans., *The Isaiah Targum, The Aramaic Bible II*. Edinburgh: T&T Clark, 1987.

Davids, Peter H., *Commentary on James*. NIGNTC. Grand Rapids, MI: Eerdmans, 1982.

Davis, Ellen F., *Scripture, Culture, and Agriculture: An Agrarian Reading of the Bible*. Cambridge: Cambridge University Press, 2009.

Davies, William, D., and Dale C. Allison, *Matthew 1–7*. ICC. Volume 1. London: T&T Clark, 1988.

———, *Matthew 19–28*. ICC. Volume 3. London: T&T Clark, 1997.

Echlin, Edward P., *Earth Spirituality: Jesus as the Centre*. New Alresford: Arthur James Publishing, 1999.

———, *The Cosmic Circle: Jesus & Ecology*. Dublin: The Columba Press, 2004.

———, *Climate and Christ*. Dublin: Columba, 2010

Flor, Elma, "The Cosmic Christ and Ecojustice in the New Cosmos (Ephesians 1)," in N. Habel & V. Balabanski (eds.), *The Earth Story in the New Testament*. Earth Bible 5. Sheffield: Continuum, 2002: 137–47.

Fretheim, Terence E., "The Plagues as Ecological Signs of Historical Disaster," *Journal of Biblical Literature* 110; 1991: 385–96.

Freyne, Sean, *Jesus, a Jewish Galilean: a New Reading of the Jesus-Story*. London: T&T Clark, 2004.

Gorman, Michael J., *Cruciformity: Paul's Narrative Spirituality of the Cross*. Grand Rapids: Eerdmans, 2001.

———, Michael J., *Reading Paul*. Milton Keynes: Paternoster, 2008.

Gorringe, Timothy, *The Sign of Love: Reflections on the Eucharist*. London: SPCK, 1997.

Gundry, Robert, *Matthew*. 2nd ed. Grand Rapids, MI: Eerdmans, 1994.

Harrington, Daniel, and Donald P. Senior, *1 Peter; Jude and 2 Peter*. Sacra Pagina 15. Collegeville, Minnesota: Liturgical Press, 2003.

Hartin, Patrick J., *James*. Sacra Pagina 14. Collegeville, Minnesota: Liturgical Press, 2003.

Hauerwas, Stanley, "Sex in Public: How Adventurous Christians Are Doing It," in J. Berkman and M. Cartwright (eds.), *The Hauerwas Reader*. Durham and London: Duke University Press, 2001: 481–504.

Hays, Richard B., *The Moral Vision of the New Testament: A Contemporary Introduction to New Testament Ethics*. London: Continuum T&T Clark, 1997.

Hayter, Teresa, *The Creation of World Poverty: An Alternative View to the Brandt Report*. London: Pluto Press, 1982.

Hopkins, Robert, *The Transition Handbook: From Oil Dependency to Local Resilience*. Devon, UK: Green Books, 2008.

Horsley, Richard A., *Jesus and the Spiral of Violence*. Minneapolis: Fortress Press, 1993.

———, *Jesus and Empire: The Kingdom of God and the New World Disorder*. Minneapolis: Fortress Press, 2003.

Jeremias, Joachim, *Jesus's Promise to the Nations*. Studies in Biblical Theology 24. Naperville, IL: Alec R. Allenson, 1958.

Jones, James, *Jesus and the Earth*. London: SPCK, 2003.

Kavanaugh, John F., *Following Christ in a Consumer Society*. Maryknoll, New York: Orbis Books, 1981.

Kraybill, Nelson, *Imperial Cult and Commerce in John's Apocalypse*. JSNTSup. 132. Sheffield: Sheffield University Press, 1996.

Lane, John, *Timeless Simplicity*. Devon, UK: Green Books, 2001.

Larrson, Goran, *Bound for Freedom: A Book of Exodus in Jewish Christian Tradition*. Peabody, MA: Hendrickson, 1999.

Laws, Sophie, *A Commentary on the Epistle of James*. Black New Testament Commentaries. London: Adam & Charles Black, 1980.

Leech, Kenneth, *True Prayer*. London: Sheldon Press, 1980.

Leske, Adrian M., "Human Anxiety and the Natural World," in N. Habel & V. Balabanski (eds.), *The Earth Story in the New Testament*. Earth Bible 5. Sheffield: Continuum, 2002: 15–27.

Loader, William, "Good News—for the Earth? Reflections on Mark 1:1–15," in N. Habel & V. Balabanski (eds.), *The Earth Story in the New Testament*. Earth Bible 5. Sheffield: Continuum, 2002: 28–43.

Lohfink, Norbert F., *Option for the Poor: The Basic Principle of Liberation Theology in the Light of the Bible*. Berkeley: BIBAL Press, 1987.

Lucas, Ernest, "The New Testament Teaching on the Environment," *Transformation* 16:3; 1999: 93–99.

Maathai, Wangari, *Unbowed: One Woman's Story*. London: Arrow Press, 2008.

MacDaniel, Jay B. (ed.), *Liberating Life: Contemporary Approaches to Ecological Theology*. Maryknoll, NY: Orbis Books, 1990.

Maier, Harry O., "There Is a New World Coming! Reading the Apocalypse in the Shadow of the Canadian Rockies," in N. Habel & V. Balabanski (eds.), *The Earth Story in the New Testament*. Earth Bible 5. Sheffield: Continuum, 2002: 166–79.

Marlow, Hillary, "Justice for All the Earth: Society, Ecology and the Biblical Prophets" in R. S. White (ed.), *Creation in Crisis*. London: SPCK, 2009: 192–208.

Marshall, Christopher, *The Little Book of Biblical Justice*. Intercourse, PA: Good Books, 2005.

Martin, Ralph, *James*. Word Biblical Commentary 48. Waco, TX: Word Books, 1988.

McDonagh, Seán, *To Care for the Earth*. London: Geoffrey Chapman, 1986.

———, *Greening the Christian Millennium*. Dublin: Dominican Publications, 2000.

Moltmann, Jürgen, *God in Creation*. London: SCM, 1985.

Moo, Douglas, "Creation and New Creation," in R. S. White (ed.), *Creation in Crisis*. London: SPCK, 2009: 241–54.

Moo, Jonathan, "Environmental Unsustainability and a Biblical Vision of the Earth's Future," in R. S. White (ed.), *Creation in Crisis*. London: SPCK, 2009: 255–70.

Morris, Leon, *Revelation*. Tyndale New Testament Commentaries. Leicester: IVP, 1969.

Murray, Robert, "The Relationship of Creatures within the Cosmic Covenant," *Month*, November 1990: 425–32.

———, *The Cosmic Covenant: Biblical Themes of Justice, Peace and Integrity of Creation*. London: Sheed & Ward, 1992.

Nolland, John, *Luke 1–9:20*. Word Biblical Commentary 35a. Dallas, TX: Word Books, 1989.

Northcott, M. S., *The Environment and Christian Ethics*. Cambridge: CUP, 1996.

———, *A Moral Climate: The Ethics of Global Warming*. London: DLT, 2007.

Padilla, C. René, "Globalization, Ecology and Poverty" in R. S. White (ed.), *Creation in Crisis*. London: SPCK, 2009: 175–91.

Pennington, Jonathan, *Heaven and Earth in the Gospel of Matthew*. Grand Rapids, MI: Baker Academic, 2007.

Ringe, Sharon H., *Jesus, Liberation, and the Biblical Jubilee*. Eugene: Wipf&Stock, 1985.

Rossing, Barbara R., "River of Life in God's New Jerusalem: An Eschatological Vision for Earth's Future," in R. R. Ruether and D. Hessel (eds.), *Christianity and Ecology,*. Cambridge, MA: Harvard University Press; Center for World Religions, 1999: 205–24.

———, *The Rapture Exposed: The Message of the Hope in the Book of Revelation*. New York: Basic Books, 2004.

Rowland, Christopher, *Revelation*. Epworth Commentaries. London: Epworth Press, 1993.

———, "Apocalyptic, the Poor, and the Gospel of Matthew," *Journal of Theological Studies* 45; 1994: 504–18.

Ruiz, Jean-Pierre, "Taking a Stand on the Sand of the Seashore: A Postcolonial Exploration of Revelation 13," in D. L. Barr (ed.), *Reading the Book of Revelation*. Atlanta, GA: SBL, 2003: 119–35.

Selby, Peter, *Grace and Mortgage*. London: DLT, 1997.

Sen, Amartyr, *Development as Freedom*, Oxford: OUP, 1999

Sider, Ronald J., "Biblical Foundations for Creation Care," in R. J. Berry (ed.), *The Care of Creation*. Leicester, UK: IVP, 2000: 43–49.

Smith, David W., *Against the Stream: Christianity and Mission in an Age of Globalization*. Leicester, UK: IVP, 2003.

Stassen, Glen H., *Living the Sermon on the Mount*. San Francisco, CA: Jossey-Bass, 2006.

Swartley, Willard M., *Covenant of Peace: The Missing Peace in New Testament Theology and Ethics*. Grand Rapids, MI/Cambridge: Eerdmans, 2006.

Sweet, John, *Revelation*. London: SCM, 1979.

Swinton, John, and Esther Mcintosh, "Persons in Relation: The Care of Persons with Learning Disabilities," *Theology Today* 157; 2000-1: 175–84.

Tamez, Elsa, *The Scandalous Message of James*. New York: A Crossroad Book, 2002.

Trocmé, André, *Jesus and the Nonviolent Revolution*. Maryknoll, New York: Orbis Books, 2003.

Tuttle, William, "What Then Should We Eat?" *Resurgence* 252; 2008: 38–40.

Valerio, Ruth, "Chainsaws, Planes, and Komodo Dragons: Globalisation and the Environment" in R. Tiplady (ed.), *One World or Many? The Impact of Globalisation on Mission*. Pasadena, CA: William Carey Library, 2003: 105–22.

Wasley, Andrew, "On the Frontline," *Ecologist*. April 2009.

Weiser, Artur, *The Psalms*. Old Testament Library. London: SCM, 1962.

White, Robert S., "Natural Disasters: Acts of God or Results of Human Folly?" in R. S. White (ed.), *Creation in Crisis*. London: SPCK, 2009: 102–21.

Wink, Walter, *Engaging the Powers*. Minneapolis: Fortress Press, 1992.

Wittenberg, Gunther H., "The Vision of Land in Jeremiah 32," in N. Habel (ed.), *The Earth Story in the Psalms and the Prophets*. Earth Bible 4. Sheffield: Sheffield Academic Press, 2001.

Woods, Richard, "Seven Bowls of Wrath: The Ecological Relevance of Revelation," *Biblical Theology Bulletin* 38.2; 2008: 64–75.

Wright, Christopher J. H., *Old Testament Ethics for the People of God*. Leicester: IVP, 2004.

Wright, N. T., *Jesus and the Victory of God*. London: SPCK, 1996.

———, *The Resurrection of the Son of God*. London: SPCK, 2003.

Yoder, John Howard, *The Politics of Jesus*. Grand Rapids, MI: Eerdmans, 1972.

Yoder, Perry, *Shalom*. London: Spire, 1987.

www.ingramcontent.com/pod-product-compliance
Lightning Source LLC
Chambersburg PA
CBHW020654230426
43665CB00008B/430